THE DISCIPLINING OF EDUCATION
NEW LANGUAGES OF POWER AND RESISTANCE

Discourse Power Resistance Volume 2

The Disciplining of Education

NEW LANGUAGES OF POWER AND RESISTANCE

edited by Jerome Satterthwaite,
Elizabeth Atkinson and Wendy Martin

Trentham Books
Stoke on Trent, UK and Sterling, USA

Trentham Books Limited

Westview House	22883 Quicksilver Drive
734 London Road	Sterling
Oakhill	VA 20166-2012
Stoke on Trent	USA
Staffordshire	
England ST4 5NP	

First published 2004

British Library Cataloguing-in-Publication Data
A catalogue record for this book is available from the British Library

1 85856 337 2

Acknowledgements
James Avis (2003) Re-thinking trust in a performative culture: the case of education, *Journal of Education Policy* 18(3): 315-332, Taylor and Francis, revised and reprinted by permission of Taylor and Francis.

Patti Lather (2004) This *IS* your father's paradigm: government intrusion and the case of qualitative research in education, *Qualitative Inquiry* 10(1): 15-34, Sage Publications, revised and reprinted by permission of Sage Publications, Inc.

Designed and typeset by Trentham Print Design Ltd., Chester and printed in Great Britain by Cromwell Press Ltd, Wiltshire.

Contents

PART THREE
NEW MOVES: WIDENING PARTICIPATION

Discourse Power Resistance Series

SERIES EDITORS:
JEROME SATTERTHWAITE AND ELIZABETH ATKINSON

In the Spring of 2002, the first international Discourse Power Resistance conference was held in Plymouth, UK, to examine pressing issues in contemporary education. Key debates from this conference were brought together in our first book, *Discourse Power Resistance: challenging the rhetoric of contemporary education*, published in the Spring of 2003. The second conference on this theme, already fondly known as 'DPR', had given rise to two further books, presenting powerful analyses of global moves in education and offering rich and varied forms of resistance to them. Together, these three books form the opening titles in the new *Discourse Power Resistance* book series, published by Trentham. This series, which is intended for students, teachers, trainers, lecturers, researchers and those responsible for shaping educational policy, aims to promote a radical rethinking of educational theory and practice, to offer a sustained and thoughtful challenge to the *status quo* in education and to put forward positive and exciting alternatives.

Other titles in the series

Discourse Power Resistance: challenging the rhetoric of contemporary education (2003) edited by Jerome Satterthwaite, Elizabeth Atkinson and Ken Gale

Educational Counter-Cultures: Confrontations, Images, Vision (2004) edited by Jerome Satterthwaite, Elizabeth Atkinson and Wendy Martin

Introduction

JEROME SATTERTHWAITE

Looking at contemporary education in the United States, the United Kingdom and world-wide, it is difficult to exaggerate the seriousness of the gap that separates official thinking from the values, beliefs and practices of those actually engaged in learning and teaching. Official policy appears in the regulations – and the régimes for monitoring their proper observance – of increasingly prescriptive political paymasters, whose concern is to produce a workforce who will do the business, and a citizenry who will, give or take a few murmurs here and there, unquestioningly obey the law. To produce and maintain conformity of this kind is the 'Disciplining of Education'. The 'New Languages of Power' appear in the apparatus of surveillance, with the switching on and off of funding that follows the evaluation of performance.

Resistance to official policy is less easy to identify: there are so many ways, some blatant, some subtle, of challenging authority or evading capture.

Part 1, *Discipline, Direction, Control*, sets out a forthright analysis of the political context in which contemporary education operates. No attempt is made by the authors to gloss over the brutal realities or to mask the sense of anger and frustration with which learners, teachers and researchers have responded to the new directions dictated by those in power. The conditions established for the creation of new knowledge and the way that knowledge is used to further the purposes of learning and teaching, are thoroughly examined. It is a bleak account; but the authors of these chapters refuse to despair; they suggest a range of strategies for countering the dominant thinking in contemporary educational politics.

Part 2, *Case Studies*, looks in some detail at four examples of educational practice, in each of which there is a bad fit between government prescription and the lived experience of learners and teachers day by day. These chapters are there to convince the readers – and these, we must hope, will include policy makers and managers as well as practitioners – that the 'disciplining of education' simply does not work. It fails because the direction and control established by authority miss the point: decision-makers have agendas which get in the way of the serious concerns of learning and teaching.

Part 3, *New Moves, Widening Participation*, looks at five examples of students' perceptions of themselves as learners, asking how it is that students see themselves the way they do. Is poor self-esteem something contemporary culture encourages and contemporary education theory endorses? Are we being trained to think and feel frail and needy by educational theories and practices which effectively put a stop to learning? Are the dominant metaphors of learning cramping the imagination of learners so that they understand themselves and their learning in restrictive ways? These issues are explored through the careful analysis of language, and a corresponding revisioning of education proposed, through the deployment of alternative metaphor and imagery.

PART ONE
DISCIPLINE, DIRECTION, CONTROL

1

Ending educational research, countering dystopian futures

IAN STRONACH

This chapter scornfully rejects the proposals set out in the UK Government's recent White Paper, which, Stronach argues, will effectively destroy educational research in the United Kingdom as it is currently understood. Research in education is set to become the prerogative of an élite academic group which will ensure the privileging of educational élitism. Stronach relentlessly exposes the elements of fantasy, mythmaking and willful delusion which have been adduced in support of this shift in policy, which is helping to bring about what he calls the 'creeping totalitarianism of the global educational spectacle'. His chapter sets the tone of radical challenge which is maintained throughout Part 1.

O Thou that in the heavens does dwell
Wha as it pleases best Thysel,
Sends ane to heaven an' ten to hell
A' for thy greater glory
And no for onie guid or ill
They've done afore Thee!
I bless an' praise thy matchless might
When thousands Thou has left in night...
('Holy Willie's Prayer', *Poems and Songs of Robert Burns*)

END 1

End 1 is illustrated by the UK government's recent proposal in the White Paper *The Future of Education* (HMSO, 2003) to end funding support for educational research in most universities. The dust has not quite settled yet but the final score looks something like this:

Missing, presumed dead	Missing in action
(RAE scores 1-3A): 50 institutions	(RAE score 4): 19
Everlasting Life (RAE scores 5,5*,6*): 14	

Fifty institutions will receive no finance to support research. Some of the 19 may qualify as 'rising' 4s, most will not. The élite 5s will receive more, sometimes much more, funding. This is the brutal triage of the RAE endgame. It is based on ending the research development ambitions of the post-1992 universities. After ten years of successful development they are told to go back to teaching and to leave research to the 'best universities'. Bassey anticipates therefore the metaphorical death of 700 educational researchers (Bassey, 2003:30). This is ending as stasis, as final solution. And a triumph for the Elect[1]. It is also an ending that Borges anticipated in his wonderful short story 'The Lottery'. In that story the Company first set up a society run on the principles of a lottery, where all social motivations were based on the prospect that only winners would be rewarded. Then, when interest flagged, they introduced a second and accompanying motivational economy. Not only would the winners win (cf Russell Group), but they could allocate punishments to the losers (in our case operating pseudo-representatively through élitist institutions like the ESRC and HEFCE, as well as government fiat). In Borges' story, such arbitrariness was obscured by a magic that similarly asserted such transient chance as an indication of enduring virtue. And in our case it followed that capacity-building necessarily involved massive capacity-cutting; that only centralisation could guarantee excellence; that the accompanying hierarchies were permanent as well as valid and virtuous; and of course quantitatively objective in nature:

> All that is necessary to reduce the whole of nature to laws similar to those which Newton discovered, is to have sufficient numbers of observations and a mathematics that is complex enough (de Condorcet, cited by Fuller, 1999: 162)

In order that the Elect be saved, the rest must be damned. Lest the illogics of that Calvinist reduction seem too extreme a representation of the situation, let me add that Dave Hustler and I (as current editors) looked at the *British Educational Research Journal's* publications for the last seven years[2]. We then wrote to various educational media:

> The Editor
>
> We are writing in our capacity as Editors of the *British Educational Research Journal*. The journal is blind refereed, recognised by the US Social Science Citation Index, and is the premier educational research journal in the UK.
>
> To assess the impact of the proposed changes in support for research across the university sector, we examined the institutional location of all authors during our 7-year editorship. 43% came from institutions currently rated '5' or above in the RAE. 50% came from institutions rated '4' or below. 7% came from joint authors who combined these statuses.
>
> The message is clear. In terms of high quality publication, the proposed changes will half the 'research capacity' that the government believes itself to be promoting elsewhere. A real weapon of mass destruction at last[3]?
>
> Yours sincerely

The *Times Higher Education Supplement* wouldn't publish it. The *Guardian* wouldn't publish it. *Research Intelligence* didn't have enough space for it. For god's sake.

END 2

> Yet I am here, a chosen sample
> To show Thy grace is great and ample
> ('Holy Willie's Prayer', *Poems and Songs of Robert Burns*)

If End 1 is an arbitrary Calvinist separation of the saved from the damned, then End 2 is a theory of the Elect. Why are some to be raised up and others 'embedded in their regional economies' (White Paper, 2003:36)? The reasons work round a familiar 'end of ideology' resolution of global capitalism.

First, an old friend: mythicised economic instrumentalism. Here is a university system reduced to the crudest of vocationalist ambitions. Its White Paper 'vision' is a 'higher education sector which meets the needs of the economy in terms of trained people, research, and technology transfer' (*ibid.*:21). Its expressed 'values' are overwhelmingly instrumental; in three short paragraphs the report values economic well-being, skilling the nation, powering the economy, serving the public, becoming competitive, stimulating innovation, supporting productivity, benefiting society, and overall thereby avoiding the unacceptable risk of economic decline (*ibid*.10). Leaving aside the philistine nature of such a listing of 'values' ('vulgar' in the newly patrician lexicon of ex-Thatcherite Chris Patton, *Observer* 29 June, 2003), it is impossible to posit a direct articulation of the university sector to economic need without ending up in some Stalinist farce of forward planning[4]. Yet the 'cure' is just that kind of direct connection: Employer 'needs', 'Work Experience', 'employability skills', 'personal developmental portfolios', business involvement in the curriculum, quality, audits and the promise of much added value... TVEI's back in town! And with the same cast of clowns[5].

Later we will look more closely at these forms of ending. Their dynamics are different but they are related in interesting ways. They combine ruthless and arbitrary selection (in terms of educational futures as opposed to current 'comparisons'), vocationalist fantasy, allied to absurd assumptions about the nature of Educational Research as a Failing Science (cf 'failing' schools, 'failing' states[6] etc) and the alleged need for research everywhere to be patterned on some ill-considered notion of Big Science.

The White Paper repeatedly conflates 'research' with a version of 'science'. Most notably: 'Looking at Nobel prizes, or at citation rates for scientists... indicates that although our position is still strong it is declining' (*ibid*.:13). But the 44 Nobel Prize winners it enumerates are not a valid performance indicator across all the disciplines in the university sector so much as they are a newspaper headline. This Government frequently mistakes newspaper headlines for performance indicators; and its other indicators are almost as dubious – 'research expenditure per patent', 'citation rates for scientists' (*ibid*.15,13). The Arts, Humanities, Social Sciences and the numerous Professional Studies such as Education and Social Work appear as asides, or not at all, assumed to be amenable to the same sorts of developmental prescriptions as 'Science'.

> ..totalitarianism appears to be only the last stage in a process during which [here Arendt cites Voegelin's 'The Origins of Scientism', 1948] science has become an idol that will magically cure the evils of existence and transform the nature of man (Arendt, 1951: 346)

In Education, for example, it is impossible to work with teachers (in ITE or CPD) towards a research-informed redefinition of professional practice without teaching and research developing a close and synergetic relationship. The 'cutting edge' is sometimes at the centre, the interface between research and professional practice, rather than some imagined peripheral frontier. Nor is that an idiosyncrasy of Education, and so it is the professional future of many of our public services that the White Paper undermines.

Having made its misdiagnoses and set Polanyi spinning in his grave, the White Paper moves on to advocate a universalist solution: more selectivity between universities, bigger groups of researchers, world class centres. It concludes that 'modern research is less amenable to the 'lone scholar' model'. This of course is nonsense in relation to many disciplines – would a posse of historians do better? a tribe of anthropologists?

> It is really against the effects of a power of a discourse that is considered to be scientific that the genealogy [as anti-science] must wage its struggle (Foucault *Power/Knowledge*, 1980, cited in Cheater, 1999: 4)

Taken together, what is enacted by the White Paper is a kind of Fantasy Economics imposed on a crude notion of Knowledge-as-Science, and cemented with a Big-is-Beautiful rationale. From an epistemological perspective it's like watching a child play Lego with a hammer and a chisel. Much of the UK government's behaviour, of course, is plain stupid. But we should note that these 'endings' are socially strategic even when they are educationally extremely naïve. When politicians seek to reproduce privilege and hierarchy, they often raise the diversionary cry to 'break the cycle of low esteem'. (White Paper 2003: 8, 9, 18, 54, 68; see also YOP, YTS, New Apprenticeships, TVEI). Here it is a 'cunning plan' for Foundation Degrees – of equal esteem with the rest of course – and an Access Regulator to make more egalitarian those 'best' institutions that are at the same time and within the same policy framework being made more élitist and inaccessible. We should not under-estimate the phoney flair of Tony Blair: New Labour, New Baldrick.

END 3

> Lord bless Thy chosen in this place,
> For here thou has a chosen race!
> ('Holy Willie's Prayer', *Poems and Songs of Robert Burns*)

It would be a hard-headed totalitarianism that said: this is what you must do. It would be a soft-headed totalitarianism that tried to[7]. It follows that this End 3 enacts the possibilities of reform, of equality, of innovation and experimentation in order to determine and realise Best Practices, Key Stages, Added Values, Best Values, etc. Modernisation is the Key. If the last two 'Ends' were forms of stasis, of 'fixing', this End 3 must appear to be the opposite. It conjures a mobilisation of values, the instantiation of a 'libidinal economy' (Deleuze and Guattari, 1988), an endless circulation of alternatives, a kaleidoscopic 'flux' of 'improvements' that are never transformative, reforms that never quite 're-form', and so on.

Although reforms as envisaged in documents such as the recent White Paper on Higher Education appear definitive, a more historical and broader location of such proposals suggests their recurrent and cyclical nature. There are at least two ways of understanding this sort of circulation. The first is through the notion of 'policy hysteria' which we earlier characterised as having the following features:

- shortened cycles of reforms
- multiple innovations
- frequent policy switches
- tendency for reforms to become more symbolic in nature
- scapegoating of systems, professionals and client groups
- shifting meanings within the central vocabulary of reform
- erosion of professional discretion by centralising control
- untested and untestable success claims (Stronach and Morris, 1994)

These features were originally held to apply to policy development in Scottish education in the early 1990s. But they seem a permanent feature of contemporary modernisation drives by the New Labour government, and indeed similar theories have been developed in the

US in relation to recurrent changes in business philosophies and practices – aptly named 'fad theory' (Strang and Macy, 2001). In a quantitative study of the rise of the Quality Control movement, Strang and Macy identify a clear pattern:

1. A potentially extensive incubation period where few firms utilise the innovation.

2. A take-off period where popularity rises explosively.

3. A short period of ascendancy marked by very high levels of innovation usage.

4. A period of rapid decline leading to a low equilibrium level of usage (2001:151)

They reach a number of conclusions that illuminate policy hysteria. First they suggest 'that a preoccupation with performance can paradoxically generate waves of adoption of innovations that are worthless, or nearly so, followed by waves of abandonment' (*ibid.* 155). They reach the conclusion that 'an artificial world of actors preoccupied with performance via success stories is a world of fad-like waves of adoption and abandonment' (*ibid.*162), and refine these findings with the claim that 'fadlike vicissitudes are most robust *not* (their emphasis) when innovations are worthless but when they have identifiable but modest merit' (*ibid.*172). In this sort of scenario the elements of fix and flux can each be seen as the dynamic of the other, combining performative realities with representational fallacies. As such, these tend to permanently 'disorder' the 'economies of performance' that constitute the public estimation of the worth of professional performances in an audit culture (Stronach *et al*, 2002). Little wonder that contemporary professional performances are so often split, critical, agonistic, inauthentic and compromised. This is not to argue forward to a utopian resolution, nor to a nostalgic recovery of illusory holism. It is to argue for a different kind of strategy, in terms of a critical reflexivity and an avowedly conflictual sense of professionalism and political engagement. Of which more later.

If we look briefly over these three different sorts of endings we can see that they are an odd mixture of 'fix' and 'flux'. Substantively, they assert endings, resolutions, solutions. They are destinations. But methodologically, they are operationalised within an evanescent flux of initiatives, documents, papers, tasks, claims, etc. relying more on amnesia than on memory for their persuasiveness, and on 'improvement' symbolism rather than resource change. They instantiate the 'hyperreal' in Baudrillard's terms[8]. Those things claiming to 'fix' are always in motion: those things alleged to be in movement are never in motion – in the terms in which they promise. Fix and flux silently change place. They are, in that sense, the very opposite of the 'evidence-based' policy they currently invoke – the Latest Fix – because they rely not on evidence but on symbolic manipulation. They construct fictive but persuasive educational scenarios that can be mediated via league tables through a complicit media[9] to a hopefully gullible public.

It is to a consideration of these post modern realities of current mediatised educational discourse that we now turn, and in particular to their interwoven dynamics. It is a complex business understanding the oversimplification of policy, in order to get at the cultural construction of contemporary stupidity. But we must make that effort if such cycles are to be broken and turned against themselves.

Provoking the libidinal economy, or what makes governments stupid?

> O Lord! Yestreen, Thou kens, wi' Meg -
> Thy pardon I sincerely beg-
> O, may't ne'er be a living plague
> To my dishonour!
> An' I'll ne'er lift a lawless leg
> Again upon her.
> ('Holy Willie's Prayer', *Poems and Songs of Robert Burns*)

The purpose of this section of the argument is to deconstruct an aspect of the libidinal economy of a global capitalism. It will show how a series of transmutations takes place: from the material to the sexual symbolic; from object to commodity; from commodity to logo; from event to spectacle, and so on. In so doing, the construction of motivation is addressed. In particular, it is important to see how the government *fails* directly to serve or build competitiveness in the global economy. Instead, it apes the global economy's sense of space, its competitive rhetorics, asserts its worth and inevitability, and produces its mythic potential for equity through allegedly equal opportunities to compete. In other words, it constructs – without much guile, it should be said – a simulacrum of educational global competition expressed as a spectacle that further acts as a global cargo cult for capitalism itself. That cult is fantasy. It is myth. It does not work and will not ever work in instrumental terms. But it has a certain bizarre functionalism. In order to begin to understand the workings of this machine we need to understand the nature of the specific capillaries through which it excites desire.

Our first analogy might be labelled A Street Car Named Desire.

Look at, for instance, an Alpha Romeo advertisement. It is about a kind of 'magic pornography' in the contemporary world. Not magic in the peripheral and traditional senses, located in superstition or religion. But the everyday, global, capitalist transmutation of objects into symbols, symbols into motivation and behaviour – the excitation of an economy of desire. Based not on need, but on the construction of want – the provocation of desires. The dynamic I have in mind can be seen in the transforming of objects (eg: 'car') into commodities (logo – badge without a body) via symbolism (sexual commodity – body without a head). The Alfa Romeo advertisement provokes an interplay of radiator grilles with the similarly 'barred/bared' breasts of a juxtaposed model. The distinctively heart-shaped grille of the car frames sex with that ancient roman symbol of desire and sets the logo astir with resonations (Alfa/alpha male; Roméo/Rómeo). The car is blacked out: the car as object does not appear. That is their intercourse, while the slogan rhymes: 'Stir your Soul'[10].

What's this got to do with 'education' in a libidinal economy? I want to argue that there are similar processes through which everyday subjects, like 'pupils', are transmuted – by numbers – into symbolic objects of value and set in motion in an economy of desire. The commodification of the woman is paralleled by the commodification of the pupil, and of education itself. Both are arranged to provoke a libidinal economy of desires. 'Best Car'? 'Best Value', 'World Class'[11]? These 'objective' and 'concrete' provocations of value (SATs, national league tables, TIMSS[12], etc) are also, then, a form of contemporary magic – and a pornography[13] – which apes the structuring motivations of the global capitalist economy. The league table is the radiator grille – a template of desire. Far from such tables of 'educational outcomes' offering the most objective account of comparative effectiveness, that acme of modernist aspirations, they advertise a bizarre spectacle of education as a symbolic discourse of reductive appearances and false comparisons – and invite a form of consumption that Little has defined as post modern: 'self-realisation through the consumption of signs' (Little, 1993:12). *We* become our league table position, and we want to be 'on top' – in both examples. At any rate, numbers construct a neocapitalism of the self. In this process of de-education the individual is blacked out, along with the purposes and processes of education, and the whole sociology of educational differences. Such discourses, therefore, are real, but only in their effects. And in that self-realisation – a provocative traffic in images of performance – it is the quantitative expression of education that is decisively motivating: what stirs the soul in this instance is the re-expression of size as position in the league table. All questions of value are swept into the vortex of a single concern: are we winning or losing? (the woman, the car, the man, the education race, the economic competition, the polls...)

Here I address only international comparisons and focus on the results of the Third International Maths and Science Study (TIMSS). They construct the only 'world' in which calls for education to be 'world class' can make sense. Position Matters! 'Our goal is to lead all other countries in the achievement of our pupils in mathematic and science' (USA) (TIMSS, 1998); or: 'English Year 9 Maths performances were significantly lower than those of students in about half of the 41 countries that took part in the survey' (Harris, 1998). In this kind of effectiveness imperative, education is performed, normed and publicised as a global audit based on the hard sciences of testing and statistics and justified as a necessary preparation for successful global competition. It inserts the legitimacy of a meritocratic myth to disguise the much more structural and historically regressive inequities of global capitalism. And, although it is nonsense, it doesn't *do* nonsense.

How is the myth performed and made credible? After all, it offers a circular argument, where league position becomes purpose, and purpose makes astonishing metaphorical leaps. The 'Year 9 English child' expresses the whole nation as a Collective Individual. The test item stands for the whole notion and purpose of education, thereby bringing about the accidental death of educational philosophy – the purposes of education being reduced to doing better than the rest.

Education stands for the economy. These multiple *synecdoche* (meta-phor where part stands for the whole) offer a shaky edifice of mixed metaphors and dodgy reductionism, mathematised and correlated so that figures of speech are magically transmuted into a speech of figures.

The global world of educational comparisons can be viewed as a highly mythic representation of a country's comparative educational performance. In relation to our initial analogy, numbers become the New Sex through which the templates of educational desire are con-structed. And far from representing educational reality they re-present educational discourse as a global anthropological spectacle. How so? They offer a 'public display of society's central and meaningful elements' (Beeman, 1993: 380), become 'obligatory passage points' through which debate must pass (Latour, 1993), draw on the 'emic appeal of league tables' (Edelman, 1988: 17) in a simultaneously crazy and common sense evaluation of educational merit. All of this fits well with Debord's notion of the 'society of the spectacle'.

McAloon studies another kind of contemporary spectacle, the modern Olympic Games. Ironic analogies have been drawn between TIMSS and the Olympics by a number of commentators but here no irony is intended. Just as the Olympics are a mixture of philosophy, games, ritual, festival and spectacle, so too is TIMSS, as a cultural per-formance, a mixture of myth, cargo cult, philosophy, ritual and spec-tacle. Both are, in McAloon's terms 'neoliminal events' (MacAloon, 1988) characteristic of our times. But they ought to have even more in common, since De Coubertin defined the goal of the modern Olympics as *educational*: 'delivering man from the constituting vision of *homo economicus*' (cited in MacAloon, 1984: 257). The TIMSS vision, along with other league tables and the recent White Paper, is precisely the opposite – the uncritical celebration of Economic Man. It is all educational nonsense, of course, but it effects a very useful transformation of the differentials of economic success into educa-tional inputs where all, implicitly, have an equal chance to success – as individuals or nations. And of course, it nicely lays off any econo-mic failures as an educational problem.

So what can we conclude? That number is the wand that conjures the templates of educational and economic desire. That league tables invoke the 'modern' while inhabiting the post modern. That the most powerful educational theories of our times hopelessly confuse their own invocations of rationality with ritual, mathematics with magic. That their order is deeply disordered, if highly functional in terms of symbolic capital, but not material capital, except as mythic reinforcement.

Fixing, fluxing, ending ...

> Thy strong right hand, Lord, mak it bare
> Upo' their heids
> Lord, visit them, an' dinna spare
> For their misdeeds
> ('Holy Willie's Prayer' *Poems and Songs of Robert Burns*)

So why is this educational world of ours never fixed? Why do we seem condemned forever to live in sin? In the scenarios we have considered here, the answer lies in the mythic nature of the fixes that are attempted, or perhaps it would be better to say 'performed'. Endings are constantly evoked (as Targets, Outcomes, Tables, Positions etc) and endlessly replaced or repaired (as Projects, Initiatives, Task Forces etc). And so flux and fix are never opposites in the libidinal economy. Instead, they guarantee each other. Their guarantee is written into the permanent nature of their inability to be what they say they are (a solution, a cure, an ending). They construct in this negative way both the need and desire for each other, and mobilise that libidinal economy in ways which are always in some measure self-reproductive. Position is always in need of either replication or repair. Fix and flux together perform – by being the opposite of their semantic promise – ephemeral illusions of success, or at least of problems under repair. At the same time they construct within each other the conditions for the amnesia (fast-moving, short-term, permanently innovative while innovatively impermanent measures) that will permit and require their recurrence – both as problems and as solutions. In that sense it is not surprising that the same curriculum basket of relevant reforms should re-circulate through education and training discourses. First, as youth training reforms (YOP/YTS), then as TVEI in a vocationalisation of the secondary curriculum, and finally through Higher Education as a further exercise in instrumental relevance. English education is a haunted house, with politicians, media and policy-makers as its unwitting (g)hosts.

14

Of course, this is government by cock-up rather than conspiracy. But there is conspiracy as well. The game within these various mobilisations remains a celebration – through spectacle – of global capitalism. It is a mythic and spectacularised simulation, a post modern cargo cult. But it is not simply farce. We should not just picture Blair, Blunkett, Clarke and Miliband, arms outstretched, pretending to be American B17s, or playing Trobriand cricket. This equally interminable game works well, but far from its instrumental surfaces (Economic Competitiveness, Comparative Educational Outcomes, Knowledge Economies, Productivity, etc). For in its insistent circling of the theme of global capitalism as a transcendent inevitability it describes and proscribes a certain kind of censorship of other alternatives, not least by its distracting busy-ness and acceleration of work routines. It inscribes a certain intolerance of, or indifference to, other educational goals, and therefore also of discrepant research methodologies if they depart from its favoured accountancy. It achieves this by making it difficult to find the time or space to think differently, by keeping its most vulnerable assumptions axiomatic and thus hidden from view by a speedy epistemology, rather than by censorship or direct coercion. Its 'strong right hand' epistemology (positivist, quantified, normative, punitive) re-contours change into improvement and regression scales that are inherently conservative. It seeks to make resistance unthought rather than unthinkable. And it therefore provokes ameliorative discourses of 'improvement' rather than change (which is why 'enhance' has become the verb of choice in the discourse). These either propose a positivist acceptance of the epistemological circulation centred on global capitalism (effectiveness and improvement discourses; evidence-based universal prescription programmes such as EPPI), or offer realist reforms based on utopian assumptions[14].

.. and beginning
> That I am here before Thy sight
> For gifts and grace
> A burning and a shining light
> To a' this place!
> (Holy Willie's Prayer. *Poems and Songs of Robert Burns*)

A confession: I do not have an ending for this chapter because of course it has to be a beginning, and I am unsure as yet (said hopefully) what new directions resistance must take. In one sense, resistance by definition knows what it wants – the end of what it doesn't want. So the question answers itself. We should not want the creeping totalitarianism of the global educational spectacle. Nor the ways in which centralisation and élitism will narrow research, methodology, training, and professional practices in the authoritarian funnelling of an increasing state coercion. Nor should we believe their false promises of 'equal' opportunities or even of 'excellence'. We cannot gain from the 'hyperactivity' of the audit culture (Strathern, 1997: 318), nor the 'savage capitalism' it quietly screens off (Robinson, 2001:171). Certainly we must reject the New Accountancy with its stifling enumerations – reductive, simplistic, and enormously corrupting in relation to educational and social goals (Desrosières, 2001). The authoritarian rhizomes of audit régimes have to be ridiculed, their 'onion-like' characteristics exposed (Arendt, 1966:413).

But we should be optimistic about these pessimisms. The mad logics of global and national audit are cumulative and self-destructive. The stresses and strains of such coercion, of the deprofessionalisation of public services, and of managerialism are well known. None of them serves the future of global capitalism because by its own current logics it cannot have a future that is anything other than the increasing impoverishment and degradation of the world. A turnover must come, although what it looks like will not be clear until it begins to happen.

The cast of the future is many and varied. Shall we be flaneurs, angels, nomads, cyborgs, insurgents, public intellectuals, mestizas, bricoleurs, sojourners or vampires? One, some, or all? I feel uneasy about these radical identities. They conjure up the image of SS Modernity, aground on the sandbanks of postmodernity, her back broken. A diaspora of rather gaudy and self-absorbed lifeboats fan out from the wreck. Are they not all castaways in the sense that Derrida has criticised, diversely sharing the fantasy of a 'proper identity'. I think I have more faith in the aporetic, iterable, and incalculable subject (Derrida, 2001: 96). To put it another way, we need more character rather than more characterisation. Foucault (2001: 122, 171) latterly called for the 'fearless speech' of 'parrhesia', on behalf of the norm of 'provocative dialogue'. He stressed the necessary risk of such an attitude, and the singular nature of 'the history of an answer – the

16

original, specific, and singular answer – to a certain situation' (*ibid.*: 173). Swedberg puts it more simply:

> What is needed today … is a thorough discussion of the social and institutional conditions under which individuals can acquire the strength to stand up and defend their rights in difficult situations … What kind of schools, universities and corporations are needed for *civil courage* to flourish? (1999:523, his emphasis)

Certainly these are not the efficient and effective servants of global capital the White Paper has in mind. Nor are they that well-known legion of carefully conformist educational researchers bent on doing the government's will, even if grudgingly. The future has to be about productive conflict and its sensible negotiation, not about the sorts of utopian resolutions that the current literature on educational research and evaluation has in mind (Stronach, Hallsall and Hustler, 2002). Such conflict from the academic community requires a good deal more character than it has lately shown – 'no other era has worn its academic freedom more lightly, nor given it away more readily' (Stronach, 2002: 185).

So have we the dystopian courage to aim for a different identity?

Notes

1. A question to the DPR audience at Plymouth in 2003 revealed that none of the 80-odd audience were from '5' rated institutions. 'Discourse, Power, Resistance' is a radical forum – it clearly doesn't pay to be radical in the audit régime.
2. The journal is the leading general educational research publication in the UK and has a high SCCI rating internationally (23 out of 93). The 7 years were the period of our editorship (Hustler and Stronach).
3. The letter went in slightly different forms to each media outlet.
4. The White Paper confidently cites Sianesi and Reenen (2002) on the 'compelling' links between education and productivity, only footnoting possible reservations. Sianesi and Reenen are defending their own paradigm in that article, yet list a number of caveats about, for example, the possible 'bi-directional causality between human capital accumulation and economic growth' (p14), the possible contamination of correlations and causes which remain problematic (p22), the 'weakness' of the empirical evidence (p38), and the invalid and imponderable nature of many of the comparisons that have been made. Not to mention the possible 'negative growth returns of further expansion in education in developed countries'(p28). Quite why the case remains 'compelling' is not clear.
5. Thatcher launched TVEI (Technical and Vocational Education Initiative) in an attempt to vocationalise secondary schooling, especially though not only for the 'less able'. It pioneered many of these sorts of pedagogical developments, while also borrowing extensively from YTS provision. In particular it gave birth to the notions of 'added value' and 'delivery', thus intensifying the commodification of educational processes

and products. Interestingly, the notion of 'delivery' is now under attack from government minister Hewitt (BBC 4,Today programme, 4 July 2003).

6. Who or what is the archetype of success that lies behind such formulations of 'failure'? For Hargreaves *et al* it's Medical Science.

7. Arendt cites Dennis Wrong on the definition of totalitarianism: 'the penetration of social life by a hierarchically organised political-ideological movement claiming to represent the 'masses" (Arendt, 1951:176). The disciplining of educational life, processes and outcomes through Ofsted type procedures fits very well with this sort of definition, as does the plethora of accountability régimes such as QAA, RAE, SATs, CHI etc.

8. Baudrillard : 'it is rather a question of substituting signs of the real for the real itself; that is, an operation to deter every real process by its operational double, a metastable, programmatic, perfect, descriptive machine..' (1988:167)

9. In these matters at least, it is the government which is complicit with the media, and not the other way round. In particular their allegiance is to the forms of media message – to the sound bite rather than to the sound-bitten, and to the simple, clear encapsulation of complexity as a reductive and self-deceiving 'common sense'.

10. This sexual traffic in meaning is 'emancipated' by French car-makers – remember 'Size Matters', chaps.

11. UK government minister, Miliband, boasts of emerging 'world class standards' (Channel 4 News, July 16th 2003) in English schools, by which he means that teachers are more effectively teaching to the test than in the past. Such trends, their politically opportunist nature, their unsustainability, and the unfortunate costs they have for the globally untested areas of the curriculum have been usefully exposed by Ryan and others.

12. SATs are Standard Attainment assessments applied nationally in England. They offer normative appraisal of the national cohort at various 'stages' of state education. Pupils are sorted into 'levels'. Schools are thereby normed into league tables according to such results.

13. Pornography is defined by SOED as 'a dealing with the obscene' and specifically related to 'prostitutes and their patrons'. Prostitution is not 'sex' any more than league tables are 'education' or 'health'. Both are essentially a proxy, a commodification of desire that makes Desire (in the realm of the libidinal economy).

14. The attempt by Ofsted to close Summerhill School in 2000 and the ongoing struggle to prevent that offers an interesting example of this kind of elision. The Ofsted inspection was found by two separate evaluations to be wildly inaccurate and wholly indefensible, and the DfEE hastily abandoned its case.

Acronyms

DfES   – Department of Education and Skills
EPPI   – Evidence for Policy and Practice Information Co-ordinating Centre
ESRC   – Economic and Social Research Council
HEFCE   – Higher Education Funding Centre
HMSO   – Her Majesty's Stationery Office
Ofsted   – Office for Standards in Education
QAA   – Quality Assurance Agency
QCA   – Qualifications and Curriculum Authority
RAE   – Research Assessment Exercise
SOED   – Scottish Office of Education
YOP   – Youth Opportunities Programme
YTS   – Youth Training Scheme

References

Arendt, H (1966) *The origins of totalitarianism*. Harcourt New York:Brace/World Inc (1st published 1951)

Bassey (2003) If the power to pursue excellence in education were vested in teachers, research would have a key role, in *Research Intelligence*, 83, May

Barke, J (1986) (ed.) *Poems and songs of Robert Burns*. London: Fontana/Collins

Beeman, W (1993) The anthropology of theatre and spectacle, in *Annual Review of Anthropology*, 19: 59–88

Browne, A. Why we're all getting brighter, *The Observer*, 22nd April 2001.

Burawoy, M (2000) Marxism after communism, in *Theory and Society* 29(2): 151–174

Cheater, A (1999) Power in the postmodern era, in: Cheater, A (ed) *The anthropology of power. Empowerment and disempowerment in changing structures*. London: Routledge

Debord, G (tr Imrie, M) (1990) *Comments on the society of the spectacle*. London: Verso

Deleuze, G and Guattari, F (tr Massumi, B) (1988) *A Thousand Plateaux. Capitalism and schizephrenia*. London: Athlone

Desrosières, A (2001) How real are statistics? Four possible attitudes, in *Social Research* 68(2): 339–355

Edelman, M (1988) *Constructing the political spectacle*. Chicago ILL: Chicago University Press

Foucault, M (2001) (ed Pearson, J) *Fearless Speech*. LA, California: Semiotext(e)

Fuller, S (1999) Making the university fit for critical intellectuals: recovering from the ravages of the postmodern condition, in *British Educational Research Journal* 25(5): 583–595

Harris, S (1998) TIMSS. Performance assessment: strengths and weaknesses of students in England, AERA conference paper, San Diego CA, April

Latour, B (tr Porter, C) (1993) *We have never been modern*. Hemel Hempstead: Harvester

Little, K (1993) Masochism, spectacle, and the 'broken mirror' clown entrée: a note on the anthropology of performance in postmodern culture, in *Cultural Anthropology* 8(1): 117 -29

MacAloon, J (1984) (ed.) *Rite, drama, festival, spectacle. Rehearsals towards a theory of cultural performance*. Phil,PA: Institute for the Study of Human Issues

Patton, P and Smith, T (eds)(2001) *Jacques Derrida. Deconstruction engaged*. The Sydney Seminar. Sydney: Power Publications

Poster, M (ed.) (1988) *Jean Baudrillard. Selected writings*. Cambridge: Polity Press

Robinson, W (2001) Social theory and globalisation: the rise of a transnational state, in *Theory and Society* 30: 157–200

Sienesi, B and Reenen, J (2002) The returns to education: a review of the empirical macro-economic literature, in Institute of Fiscal Studies Working Paper 02/05, March

Strang, D and Macy, M (2001) In search of excellence: fads, success stories and adpative emulation, in *American Journal of Sociology* 107(1): 147–182

Strathern, M (1997) Improving ratings: audit in the British university system, in *European Review* 5(3): 1997

Stronach, I (1999a) Tests are no way to be the nation again, in *Times Educational Supplement* (Scotland), 12th November.

Stronach, I (1999b) Shouting theatre in a crowded fire: 'educational effectiveness' as cultural performance, in *Evaluation*, 5(2): 173-193

Stronach, I (2001) Numbers are not what they used to be: quantifying the qualitative as contemporary fool's gold, Invited presentation to the British Society for Research in Mathematics, Manchester, April

Stronach, I (2003) A critique of 'The Future of Education' Department for Education and Skills (Creating opportunity, releasing potential, achieving excellence), London, 2003, in Supplement to *Research Intelligence*, 83, May

Stronach, I, Corbin, B, MacNamara, O, Stark, S and Warne, T (2002) Towards an uncertain politics of professionalism: teacher and nurse identities in flux, in *Journal of Education Policy* 17(1): 109–138

Stronach, I, Halsall, R and Hustler, D (2002) Future imperfect: evaluation in dystopian times, in: Ryan, K and Schwaandt, T (eds) *Exploring evaluator role and identity*. Greenwich CT: IAP

Stronach, I and Morris, B (1994) polemical notes on educational evaluation in the age of 'policy hysteria', in *Evaluation and Research in Education* 8(1/2): 5–19

Swedberg, R (1999) Civil courage (Zivilcourage): the case of Knut Wicksell, in *Theory and Society* 28: 501–528

HMSO (2003) *The future of higher education*. White Paper, London

TIMMS (1998) Report Number 8. US National Research Center, April

2

This *IS* your father's paradigm: government intrusion and the case of qualitative research in education

PATTI LATHER

Following Stronach's analysis of intervention and constraint, Patti Lather explores recent policy moves which have privileged a narrow, scientistic approach to educational research in the US. She compares this with current interventionism in UK education policy (a theme taken up again by Newby in the next chapter) noting the ironic contrast between the narrow view of science being forced on educational researchers and the broadening of the critique of scientific method over the last forty years. Lather proposes 'three quite scandalous discourse practices' – Foucauldian policy analysis and feminist and postcolonial cultural analysis – 'to evoke the science that might be possible after the critique of science'.

This chapter seeks to make sense of the US Federal government's incursion into legislating scientific method in the realm of educational research via the 'evidence-based' movement of the last few years. In what follows, I address the many factors at play, including the Science Wars and the needs of neo-liberal states in a time of proliferating insurgent special interests, including that of conservative restoration. Also at play are academic capitalism, entrepreneurship and ambition and, with a nod to Adorno (1973, 1976) and Walter Benjamin (1968; Adorno and Benjamin, 1999), the traditions of critical theory in terms of the critique of instrumental reason. My title is a play upon an automotive advertisement from a few years back, 'This is NOT your father's Oldsmobile.'

In surveying a variety of ways this topic could be approached, I do not want to rehearse the various critiques of scientism that have arisen in the forty plus years since Thomas S. Kuhn's *The Structure of Scientific Revolutions* (1970). In taking on these latest twists and turns in governmental efforts to affect educational research, my interest is in how the federal effort to legislate scientific method might be read as a backlash against the proliferation of research approaches of the last twenty years in cultural studies, feminist methodology, radical environmentalism, ethnic studies and social studies of science. I will particularly call on the discourse practices of Foucauldian policy analysis, feminism via Luce Irigaray, and postcolonialism via Stuart Hall.

Legislating method: science for policy or policy for science?

It is an old argument that the social sciences are not to be subsumed under a natural science model. What is new is that in this moment of what Foucault terms 'our contemporaneity' (1991:40), this old argument against a unified idea of science (Galison and Stump, 1996) is being disavowed via nakedly political and self-aggrandising moves.

John Willinsky's (2001) call to broaden and deepen major federal policy statements regarding the translation of educational research into practice provided a wake-up call for me regarding movements at the federal level to legislate method. Rather ingeniously, Willinsky attaches a critical agenda to one that is decidedly instrumentalist and even shocking in its lack of attention to the last twenty years of research on why 'top-down linear' Research Development models of the 1950s and 1960s' didn't work (p7). Arguing for democratic forms of collaboration and exchange rather than 'heavy-handed intentions of driving educational practice' (p7), Willinsky foregrounds the 'productive tensions and radical challenges that mark this play of interpretations within social science research' (p7). Worried about 'research-wielding technocrats' (p9), his article so scared me that, at the annual meeting of the American Educational Research Association in 2002, I broke my usual rule of no 8am sessions to attend Ellen Lagemann's talk about her 2000 book, *An Elusive Science: The Troubling History of Educational Research*. While her talk was lovely, the discussion afterwards was not. It turned to the attempts of the US National Research Council's report (NRC, 2002) to negotiate between the federal government and the educational research community what it means to do scientific educational research.[1]

In spite of the efforts of the NRC report toward a 'big tent' of legitimate methods in educational research (Feuer, Towne and Shavelson, 2002), Lagemann seemed adrift in addressing how calls for generalisability, objectivity, replicability and a unified theory of science reinscribe a science under duress for some forty years. At an afternoon session at the conference where what I call 'the suits' were on the podium in force, I became even more aghast at the framing statement from a representative from OERI about the need for policy research that supported the present US administration's initiatives. This sort of nakedness was either strategic or naïve, and these folks didn't look naïve. I began to think that maybe I was the naïve one in assuming that the last forty years of the social critique of science might actually shape contemporary thought about policy driven research. I began to ask what is happening when at the very time there is a philosophical trend against certainty in the social sciences, 'this continual and noisy legislative activity' (Elden, 2002:146), with all of its normalising authority, is working at the federal level to discipline educational research to a narrowly defined sense of science based evidence.

During a visit to Ohio State University in the Spring of 2002, Andy Porter, past AERA President, expressed the view that trends come and go in Washington while the rest of the country gets on with its business. I do not share Dr. Porter's sanguine outlook on this matter. Whether or not the fifteen year timeline of the Strategic Education Research Programme of the National Research Council will change the face of educational research, this seems about much more than the latest trend in Washington DC. Elizabeth Atkinson (2003), for example, asks who loses when 'a nation of researchers is locked into a government policy agenda' (p8) and urges a sort of heresy against serving policy to the point where we collude in our own oppression. How can we take Atkinson's charge to heart of 'thinking outside the box' as educational research is being told what science is by bureaucrats and Congress at the very time when a more expansive definition of science is being urged in the more high status areas of academe (e.g. Goenka, 2002; Katz and Mishler, 2003)?

As the latest wave of the conservative attack on education, this kind of 'activist interventionism and expansion of the scope of government' (Shaker, 2002) gives the lie to the rhetoric of decreased federalism in the conservative restoration. Learning lessons from earlier efforts to gain control of reading research, mathematics, science, professional development and comprehensive school reform are being targeted as the next objects of 'high scientific standards' (see, for example, Shaker, 2002). With randomised field trials (RFT's) or randomised control trials (RCTs) now specified by Congress ever more frequently in effectiveness studies of federally funded programmes, the design and application of educational research has become a partisan tool, in much the same way as standardised tests have functioned for almost two decades.

In delineating the scientificity of science, while the NRC report tries to walk a fine line between a 'narrow behaviorism/positivism' and its concerns regarding the 'anything goes' of 'extreme' postmodernism (2002:24-25) it is, ultimately, what Foucault terms 'a kind of tribunal of reason' (1991:60). In spite of the report's oft repeated intentions of balance across multiple methods, objectivity is enshrined and prediction, explanation and verification override description, interpretation and discovery within the sort of research endorsed by the report (see Shavelson *et al.*, 2003). While the contested nature of science is much evoked in the report, an epistemological sovereignty is assumed in delineating and applying principles in the doing of 'high quality science.' The exclusionary force of its 'guiding principles' is striking in its disavowal of different views of evidence, analysis and purpose. Rationality's domesticating power is particularly fascinating in that the chapter on the specificities of educational research lists all that gets in the way of an engineering approach to science. Values and politics, human volition and programme variability, cultural diversity, multiple disciplinary perspectives, the import of partnerships with practitioners, even the ethical considerations of random designs: all are swept away in a unified theory of scientific advancement with its mantra of 'science is science is science' across the physical, life and social sciences. While one expects to sort through several voices in a committee prepared document, in the end its efforts to provide guidelines for rigor and enhance a 'vibrant federal presence' (p129) are complicit with the federal government's move towards evidence-based knowledge as being much more about policy for science than science for policy.

Evidence based practice: science, money and politics

With little time for Derrida and Deleuze, I buried myself in the updates on 'Bush Science' from Education Week, tried to keep up with policy analysis of these twists and turns and even developed some web access skills. I learned three things from all of this.

The British scene

The first thing I learned is that Britain has been going through this extremely interventionist regulatory climate, policed by statutory bodies for over a decade. In her introduction to an edited book in which the focus is largely on health care policy, Liz Trinder appraises strengths and weaknesses across both 'champions and critics' of evidence-based practice (Trinder, 2000:3). She theorises its appeal and, hence, its rapid influence, as rooted in the needs of post-traditional societies for ways of managing risk in the face of a paradoxical dependence on and suspicion of experts and expert knowledge. Combined with the push towards value-for-money, the rise of managerialism, consumerism and political discourses of accountability and performance, neoliberal ideologies of the neutrality of such practices prevail in an 'explosion of auditable management control systems' (p9). Here, at last, is a way to manage quality issues by displacing professional judgment with promised effectiveness via the procedural production of evidence. While it is undoubtedly 'a product of its time' (p5), the problem is that there is little evidence that evidence-based practice actually works (p2).

Hammersley notes that in medicine, the focus has been on quality of practice, whereas in education, the focus has been on the quality of research (2000:163). He also notes the focus on teaching as opposed to administration and management and how, in spite of the claims of evidence-based practice of being a 'radically new venture' (p164), research based teaching has a long history, including a long critique. The shift to qualitative methods in the 1970s led to educational research, according to Hammersley, becoming 'embroiled in philosophical and methodological disputes' (p167) that cannot be simply overcome. The degree to which the kinds of problems that teachers

25

face are open to solution by research is precisely the question. The importance of contextual judgment mandates a great caution in adapting the medical model to the field of education. Formulae for transparent accountability are more about politics than about quality of service.

For the purposes of this chapter, it is the mutations of the classic approach in the British scene that are particularly instructive. The introduction of qualitative research, the interruption of the top-down approach, the pluralistic interpretations of what is evidence: this is a sort of translation in diffusion. Calls for effectiveness studies of evidence-based practice displace the hegemony of meta-analysis and Randomised Control Trials (far less dominant in the UK than in the US in educational research, but widely used in fields such as medicine), by capitalising on the move in focus from advocacy to implementation. In nursing research, for example, given the displacement of the empiricism of the natural sciences by phenomenology and its rejection of objectivism, the eclecticism of qualitative approaches interrupt positivism dramatically enough to work as a counter force to prevailing narrow ideas of what constitutes evidence (Blomfield and Hardy, 2000).

Shore and Wright's anthropology of policy work in Britain, New Zealand and, of late, Denmark, adds a compelling layer to our understanding of these movements across time and national borders (1997; 1999; 2000; 2001). Their stories (in press) on new managerialism out of control in Australia were particularly troublesome. They provide a body of work that argues that this is less about scientific rigor and quality and more about delivering support to government policies and strengthening management control: In short, a new form of coercive and authoritarian governmentality.

Déjà vu all over again

The second thing I learned is that there are a handful of advocates well positioned to push for this scientistic approach to policy-driven research in the US (Mosteller and Boruch (eds) 2002). At root is the question of what to do about federal needs for evaluation data on educational initiatives in a time of belt-tightening economies. The good old days of the 1960s are evoked, when the federal trough was rich with programme evaluation monies as the research budget for education soared from 3 million in 1960 to 100 million in 1967 (Vivovskis, 2002:123). Foregrounding an expansive federal role in financial, political and regulatory environments, policy makers long for something like the Federal Drug Administration (FDA) to 'require good evidence' regarding which educational interventions are safe or effective. It is high time for 'rigorous evaluation' on the part of 'randomisers' to assume important positions at the federal level. 'Generating better evidence for better education' (Boruch and Mosteller, 2002: 14) is the watchword.

It is of particular interest to note how conservative think tanks have ratcheted up their focus on education issues since the late 1980's and how entrepreneurial interests are at work.[2] In *Science, Money and Politics* (2001), Daniel Greenberg probes the demands for utilitarian science versus scientific autonomy within the National Science Foundation, which he situates as a 'little dog' compared to defence, space and medical research. The 'politics of the academic pork barrel' (p184) work toward a sort of 'scientific welfare' (p39) within the Enterprise University (p356) with its grant economy, where the social sciences are insulted by being largely left out. If real science is about scepticism, curiosity and passion (p24) where transparency of process is the only agreed upon fundamental, Greenberg asks whether science could serve us better (p10) if it moved beyond its 'capacity for believing it is the victim of neglect and hostility' (p60) and its perpetual grant chasing.

It appears that science, money and politics have combined with pre-positioned capability and sweetheart contracts on the part of self-described 'ambitious researchers' (Burtless, 2002:193) to court the increased federal role in the adoption of experimental methods. As argued by Baez and Boyles (2002), in their lovely analysis of the discourse of grants, it is not that 'academic capitalism' has not become our way of life. The deal has already been struck. The question is the extent to which we can promote critical work within such a *milieu*, 'work which challenges the categories that organise [our] existence' (p45) given the Faustian bargain of the federal and corporate embrace.

Toward a policy relevant counter-science: fieldwork in philosophy

The third thing I have learned is that we need to put our critical theory to work right now. In his discussion of how conservative modernisation has radically reshaped the common sense of society regarding education, Michael Apple asks, '*If the right can do this, why can't we?*' (2001:194, original emphasis) In addressing such a question, I suggest that the Left needs a policy turn (McRobbie, 1997; Bennett, 1992; McGuigan, 2001; Ferguson and Golding, 1997), with a focus on programme evaluation as a particularly cogent site where a policy relevant counter-science might be worked out.

Making Social Science Matter (2001) by Bent Flyvbjerg, a Danish urban developer argues for a move from a narrowly defined epistemic science to a social science that integrates context-dependency with practical deliberation. Here considerations of power are brought to bear in delineating a knowledge adequate to our time. Rather than the self-defeating 'physics envy'[3] that underlies the objectivist strands of the social sciences, this is a social science that can hold its own in the Science Wars by contributing to society's practical rationality in clarifying where we are and where we want to be.

Here social science becomes a sort of laboratory toward public philosophy, what Bourdieu terms 'fieldwork in philosophy' (1990:28, from J. L. Austin, quoted in Flyvbjerg p167). Within such fieldwork, case studies assume prime importance, as critical cases, strategically chosen, provide 'far better access for policy intervention than the present social science of variables' (Flyvberg, 2001:86). In such a laboratory, against a narrow scientism in policy analysis and programme evaluation, the urgent questions become where are we going with democracy in this project? Who gains and who loses and by which mechanisms of power? Given this analysis, what should be done?

'Simultaneously sociological, political and philosophical' (Flyvberg, 2001:64), this is a science that does not divest experience of its rich ambiguity, because it stays close to the complexities and contradictions of existence. Instead of emulating the natural or, in Foucauldian terms, 'exact' sciences, the goal is getting people to no longer know what to do so that things might be done differently. This is the yes of the setting-to-work mode of post-foundational theory that faces unanswerable questions, the necessary experience of the impossible, in an effort to foster understanding, reflection and action instead of a narrow translation of research into practice.

Interrupting a discourse one finds so profoundly troubling

In the final section of this chapter, I put into play three quite scandalous discourse practices in order to explore what it might mean to dissolve the continuities of dominant narratives. I call upon the uncompromising discourses of Foucauldian policy analysis and feminist and postcolonial science to evoke the science that might be possible after the critique of science.

A Foucauldian reading[4]

In Foucauldian terms, policy is one of the three technologies of governmentality, the others being the diplomatic, the military and the economic. The purpose of policy is to regulate behaviour and render populations productive via a biopolitics that entails state intervention in and regulation of the everyday lives of citizens in a 'liberal' enough manner to minimise resistance and maximise wealth stimulation. The processes of naming, classifying and analysing all work toward disciplining through normalising. Such governmentality is 'as much about what we do to ourselves as what is done to us' (Danaher, Schirato and Webb, 2000:83). And the analysis of policy as a technology of governmentality is, contrary to the view of those who see Foucault as a pessimist and determinist, very much about how understanding such processes might raise possibilities for doing otherwise.

In *The Order of Things*, Foucault turns to the matter of the status of the human sciences. Here he argues that to look at such sciences as 'pre-paradigmatic' is to buy into some maturation narrative that belies how the human sciences are about 'constantly demystifying themselves', rather than about making themselves more precise (1970: 356, 364). Locating the human sciences in the interstices of the mathematisable and the philosophical, 'this cloudy distribution' (1970:347) is both their privilege and their precariousness. Language, meaning, the limits of consciousness, the role of representations are the stuff of human seeking to know. Rather than lacking in exactitude and rigor, the human sciences are more a 'meta-epistemological position' in being about 'finitude, relativity, and perspective' (p355). Here their very 'haziness, inexactitude and imprecision' (p355) is the form of positivity proper to the human sciences: 'blurred, intermediary and composite disciplines multiply[ing] endlessly' (p358).

In Foucault's view, the debate over whether this is truly scientific or not is a 'wearisome' discussion (1970:365). The human sciences do not answer to criteria of objectivity and systematisation, the formal criteria of a scientific form of knowledge, but they are within the positive domain of knowledge as much as any other part of the modern episteme. There is no internal deficiency here; they are not 'stranded across the threshold of scientific forms' (p366). They are not false sciences; 'they are not sciences at all' (p366). They assume the title in order to 'receive the transference of models borrowed from the sciences' (*ibid.*). Enacting 'a perpetual principle of dissatisfaction, of calling into question, of criticism and contestation' (p373), such knowledges are tied to a praxis of unmasking the representations we give to ourselves of ourselves.

In terms of the recent governing mentality of educational research, the 'privilege accorded to ... 'the sciences of man' is based on the 'political arithmetic' (Foucault, 1998:323) that makes particular kinds of discourse both possible and necessary. This is not so much about concepts on their way to formation, or even the price paid for scientific pretensions, but rather of understanding claims to scientificity as discursive events. Here the 'inexact knowledges' become *'a field of strategic possibilities'* (1998:320, original emphasis), a 'counter-science' of 'indisciplined' policy analysis that troubles what we take for granted as the good in fostering understanding, reflection and action.

A feminist reading

This militantly empiricist and quantitative movement, this desire for hardness with its claims to produce findings that are verifiable, definitive and cumulative, is set against a softness where interpretation is central and findings are always subject to debate and reinterpretation (Gherardi and Turner, 1987).

French feminist theory is premised on the idea that the classical structure is splitting and opening to becoming, and that this becoming will be initiated primarily by women as men have more to lose and their psychic structures are more called to the scene of castration

(Conley, 2000:25). Irigaray's argument (1989) that there are 'systems of thought dominated by the logic and linguistics of male sexual organs' is, of course, based on psychoanalytic theory (Olkowski, 2000:91). Her concern is that we have so naturalised such language and logic that we do not see the practical aspects of such domination. Régimes of power and systems of philosophy are designed to 'penetrate,' interventions are 'engineered', 'we encourage one another to be 'hard' on issues' (*ibid*:92). In contrast is the sort of 'embarrassing emotion-fest' of women's work (*ibid*:93) which can only be interpreted as 'excess. . . wild or crazy, bizarre, remote, or meaningless' to the task of social policy (*ibid*). What Irigaray calls 'placental economies' (1985:41) of fluid negotiation 'make us shudder' (Olkowski, 2000:96) within the 'order of good sense' (*ibid*:99). 'Disconcerting the erection of the male subject,' women's bad copies or fake science are 'an abyss in which the Father could no longer recognise himself' (p101). Proceeding by alliances, symbiosis, contagion and what Irigaray calls 'mucosity' (1993:44), this is a kind of refusal of recognition and of the proper rather than a scene of good daughters making bad copies via replication studies. Depathologising that which is associated with women, 'the uteral, the vulvar, the clitoral, the vaginal, the placental' (*ibid*) would transform the social contract and give purchase to seeing science as a site of contestation, an always already gendered practice.

A postcolonial reading

In re-reading Stuart Hall on Gramsci for the Introduction to Cultural Studies class I recently taught, I was struck with how the Right models Gramsci's tactics of a 'war of position.' Condensing a variety of different relations and practices into a definite system of rules through a series of necessary displacements, the state 'plans, urges, incites, solicits, punishes' (Hall, 1996:429).

As a sort of regressive modernism, the disciplining and normalising effort to standardise educational research in the name of quality and effectiveness is an attempt to hegemonise and appropriate to a reactionary political agenda deeper tendencies in cultural shifts. These might be termed a 'new cultural politics of difference' (Hall, 1996: 464): such a politics is marked by unevenness, contradictory outcomes, disjunctures, delays, contingencies, and uncompleted projects.

The danger of the reduction of spaces for the doing of other sorts of research on the part of a cultural dominant is that the decentering of old hierarchies and grand narratives of the last twenty or so years has created new subjects on the political and cultural stage. To try to re-inscribe a medical model of the 1970s is to set oneself up to be read as an 'aggressive resistance to difference' (Hall, 1996:468). This back-lash attempt to transfer a canonical model to educational research is an 'assault, direct and indirect, on multiculturalism' (*ibid*).

Overtaken by the carnivalesque, a sort of 'low science' has emerged out of this proliferation of difference that challenges the fundamental basis of the mechanisms of ordering and of making sense of European culture. A rich production of counter-narratives is alive and kicking, from subaltern studies to indigenous research methodologies, from native as anthropologist to Al Zazeera, the Arabic TV channel. This is the end of the innocent notion of knowledge production as value neutral. Efforts by the 'top' to reject and eliminate the 'bottom' for reasons of prestige and status bite back from a place where white masculinities are no longer at the center of the frame.

Conclusion: indisciplined knowing

To conclude, I have argued that this move at the federal level brings the Science Wars (Ross, 1996; Plotnitsky, 2002) to the realm of educa-tional research in a way much marked by the anxieties, rhetorics and practices of an imperialist and decentered masculinist régime of truth. In this, I realise that I am an enemy amidst talk of détente, the end of the paradigm wars and the call for mixed methods (Tashakkori and Teddlie, 2002). Rather than détente, however, all of this reinforces my interest in what Foucault terms 'indiscipline' as a move toward a Nietzschean sort of 'unnatural science' that leads to greater health by fostering ways of knowing that escape normativity (Nietzsche, 1974:301). By 'indiscipline,' Foucault describes a mechanism by which a marginalised population or practice is created to exert pres-sure that cannot be tolerated by the very process of exclusions and sanctions designed to guard against irregularities and infractions (Foucault 1994:36).

As an irregular trooper in the Science Wars, I see this latest round of reinscribing the idealised natural science model as an effect of power of a sort of historical amnesia that disavows decades of critique and (re)formulations toward a science after the critique of science. To think about the relation of policy and research in such a place of Foucauldian indiscipline, what I have offered might be viewed, in a Lacanian register, as 'the hysteric's discourse' (Fink 1995). Here 'a truly scientific spirit' is commanded by 'that which does not work, by that which does not fit. It does not set out to cover carefully over paradoxes and contradictions' (p134-135), like that of the master's discourse with its imperative to be obeyed within its guise of reason. The hysteric sees the heart of science as 'taking such paradoxes and contradictions as far as they can go' (p135), rather than endorsing a monolithic science 'based on a set of axiomatic mathematisable propositions, measurable empirical entities, and pure concepts' (p138).

In short, the Science Wars continue; the line between a narrowly defined scientism and a more capacious scientificity of disciplined inquiry remains very much at issue. In terms of the desirability of degrees of formalisation, mathematised or not, generic procedures, and rigorous differentiations, there is virtually no agreement among scientists, philosophers and historians as to what constitutes science except, increasingly, the view that science is, like all human endeavour, a cultural practice and practice of culture. To operate from a premise of the impossibility of satisfactory solutions means not to assume to resolve but, instead, to be prepared to meet the obduracy of the problems and obstacles as the very way toward producing different knowledge and producing knowledge differently. Foucault terms this 'the absolute optimism' of 'a thousand things to do' (1991:174), where our constant task is to struggle against the very rules of reason and practice inscribed in the effects of power of the social sciences.

This chapter is a revision of an article with the same title, published in *Qualitative Inquiry* 10 (1) 2004, 15-34 (special issue on methodological conservatism). It is reprinted by permission of Sage Publications and the editors of *Qualitative Inquiry*. The original version was written for presentation as the Guba Lecture at the annual meeting of the American Educational Research Association, Chicago, April 2003.

Notes

1   According to Daniel Greenberg (2001), the National Academy lives off of the production of 'generally dour studies' (p297), most of which are ignored. The NRC report was produced in a particularly quick schedule of six months to inform OERI reauthorisation. OERI (the Office of Educational Research and Improvement) was replaced with the Institution of Educational Sciences in the Education Reform Act of 2002.

2   These include efforts such as that of Robert Slavin, co-developer of the Success for All improvement programme at Johns Hopkins University and one of the two groups chosen by the US Department of Education in August 2002 to develop and manage a clearinghouse on 'what works in education' (w-w-c.org) and the Campbell Collaboration, based at the University of Pennsylvania and led by Robert Boruch.

3   This phrase, credited to Freud, was used in the *New York Review of Books* (Flyvbjerg, 2001, pp. 26-27). It is, interestingly, used in the NRC report, without attribution (p13).

4   From Lather (2004, in press).

References

Adorno, T (Tr Ashton, E B) (1973) *Negative Dialectics*. New York and London: Routledge and Kegan Paul

Adorno, T (ed) (1976) *The Positivist Dispute in German Sociology*. London: Heinemann

Adorno, T and Benjamin, W (1999) *The Complete Correspondence, 1928-1940* (edited by H. Lonitz) (trans. N Walker). Cambridge, MA: Harvard University Press

Apple, M (2001) *Educating the 'Right' Way: Markets, Standards, God, and Inequality*. New York: Routledge

Atkinson, E (2003) Thinking Outside the Box: An Exercise in Heresy. Paper presented at the annual meeting of the American Educational Research Association, April. (Now appearing in Qualitative Inquiry, 10(1) forthcoming, 2004: special issue on methodological conservatism.)

Baez, B and Boyles, D R (2002) Are We Selling Out? Grants, Entrepreneurship, and the Future of the Profession. Paper presented at the annual meeting of the American Educational Studies Association, October

Benjamin, W (1968) *Illuminations: Essays and Reflections* (edited by H Arendt) (trans. H Zohn) New York: Schocken

Bennett, T (1992) Putting Policy into Cultural Studies, in: Grossberg, L, Nelson, C and Treichler, P (eds) *Cultural Studies*. London: Routledge

Blomfield, R and Hardy, S (2000) Evidence-Based Nursing Practice, in: Trinder, L and Reynolds, S (eds) (2000) *Evidence-Based Practice: A Critical Appraisal*. London: Sage

Boruch, R and Mosteller, F (2002) Overview and New Directions, in: Mosteller, F and Boruch, R (eds) *Evidence Matters: Randomized Trials in Education Research*. Washington DC: The Brookings Institute

Bourdieu, P (Tr Adamson, M) (1990) *In Other Words: Essays Toward a Reflexive Sociology*. New York: Polity Press (first published in French, 1987)

Burtless, G (2002) Randomized Field Trials for Policy Evaluation: Why Not in Education?, in: Mosteller, F and Boruch, R (eds) *Evidence Matters: Randomized Trials in Education Research*. Washington DC: The Brookings Institute

Canclini, N G (2001) The North-South Dialogue on Cultural Studies, in: Canclini, N G (ed) *Consumers and Citizens: Globalization and Multicultural Conflicts*. Minneapolis: University of Minnesota Press

Conley, V (2000) Become-Woman Now, in: Buchanan, I and Colebrook, C (eds) *Deleuze and Feminist Theory*. Edinburgh: Edinburgh University Press

Cook, T D and Payne, M R (2002) Objecting to the Objections to Using Random Assignment in Educational Research, in: Mosteller, F and Boruch, R (eds) *Evidence Matters: Randomized Trials in Education Research*. Washington DC: The Brookings Institute

Danaher, G, Schirato, T and Webb, J (2000) *Understanding Foucault*. London: Sage

Elden, S (2002) The War of Races and the Constitution of the State: Foucault's Il Faut Defendre la Societe and the Politics of Calculation, *Boundary* 2, 29(1): 125-151

Ferguson, M and Golding, P (1997) Cultural Studies and Changing Times: An Introduction, in: Ferguson, M and Golding, P (eds) *Cultural Studies in Question*. London: Sage

Feuer, M J, Towne, L and Shavelson, R J (2002) Scientific Culture and Educational Research, in *Educational Researcher*, 31(8): 4-14

Fink, B (1995) *The Lacanian Subject: Between Language and Jouissance*. Princeton NJ: Princeton University Press

Flyvberg, B (2001) *Making Social Science Matter: Why Social Inquiry Fails and How it can Succeed Again*. Cambridge: Cambridge University Press

Foucault, M (1970) *The Order of Things: An Archaeology of the Human Sciences*. New York: Vintage Books (first published in French, 1966)

Foucault, M (1991) *Remarks on Marx: Conversations with Duccio Trombadori*. New York: Semiotext(e) (first published in Italian, 1981)

Foucault, M (1994) The Punitive Society, in: Rabinow, P (ed) Michel Foucault: *Ethics, Subjectivity and Truth*. Vol. 1. New York: The Free Press

Foucault, M (1998) On the Archaeology of the Sciences: Response to the Epistemology Circle, in: Faubion, J (ed) *Michel Foucault: Aesthetics, Method, and Epistemology*. Vol. 2. New York: The Free Press

Galison, P and Stump, D (eds) (1996) *The Disunity of Science: Boundaries, Contexts, and Power*. Stanford: Stanford University Press

Gherardi, S and Turner, B A (1987) *Real Men Don't Collect Soft Data*, Quarderno 13, Dipartimento di Politica Sociale, Universita di Trento

Goenka, S (2002) A Day in the Field that Changed my Methodology, in *British Medical Journal* 324:493

Greenberg, D (2001) *Science, Money and Politics: Political Triumph and Ethical Erosion*. Chicago: University of Chicago Press

Hall, S (1996) *Stuart Hall: Critical Dialogues in Cultural Studies* (edited by D. Morley and K-H. Chen). London: Routledge

Hammersley, M (2000) Evidence-Based Practice in Education and the Contribution of Educational Research, in: Trinder, L and Reynolds, S (eds) *Evidence-Based Practice: A Critical Appraisal*. London: Sage

Irigaray, L (Tr Gill, G) (1985) *Speculum of the Other Woman*. Ithaca: Cornell University Press

Irigaray, L (1989) Sexual difference, in: Moi, T (ed) *French Feminist Thought: A Reader*. Oxford: Basil Blackwell

Irigaray, L (Tr Burke, C and Gill, G) (1993) *An Ethics of Sexual Difference*. Ithaca: Cornell University Press

Kuhn, T S (1970) (2nd edn) *The Structure of Scientific Revolutions.* Chicago: University of Chicago Press

Lagemann, E (2000) *An Elusive Science: The Troubling History of Educational Research.* Cambridge, MA: Harvard University Press

Lather, P (2004) Foucauldian 'Indiscipline' as a Sort of Policy Application, in: Baker, B and Hayning, K (eds) *Dangerous Coagulations? The Uses of Foucault in the Study of Education.* New York: Peter Lang

McGuigan, J (2001) Problems of Cultural Analysis and Policy in the Information Age, in *Cultural Studies/Critical Methodologies,* 1(2): 190-219

McRobbie, A (1997) The E's and the Anti-E's: New Questions for Feminism and Cultural Studies, in: Ferguson, M and Golding, P (eds) *Cultural Studies in Question.* London: Sage

Mosteller, F and Boruch, R (eds) (2002) *Evidence Matters: Randomized Trials in Education Research.* Washington DC: The Brookings Institute

National Research Council (NRC) (2002) *Scientific Research in Education. Committee on Scientific Principles for Education Research* (edited by R J Shavelson and L Towne). Washington DC: National Academy Press

Nietzsche, F (Tr Kaufmann, W) (1974) *The Gay Science.* New York: Vintage Books (originally published in German 1887)

Olkowski, D (2000) Body, Knowledge and Becoming-Woman: Morpho-Logic in Deleuze and Irigaray, in: Buchanan, I and Colebrook, C (eds) *Deleuze and Feminist Theory.* Edinburgh: Edinburgh University Press

Plotnitsky, A (2002) *The Knowable and the Unknowable: Modern Science, Nonclassical Thought, and the 'Two Cultures.'* Ann Arbor: University of Michigan Press

Porter, T M (1995) *Trust in Numbers: The Pursuit of Objectivity in Science and Public Life.* Princeton, NJ: Princeton University Press

Ross, A (ed) (1996) *Science Wars.* Durham NC: Duke University Press

Shaker, P (2002) Is Washington Serious about Scientifically-Based Research? Paper presented at the Curriculum and Pedagogy Conference, October

Shavelson, R, Phillips, D C, Towne, L and Feuer, M (2003) On the Science of Education Design Studies, in *Educational Researcher* 32(1): 25-28

Tashakkori, A and Teddlie, C (eds) (2002) *Handbook of Mixed Methods in Social and Behavioral Research.* Thousand Oaks CA: Sage

Trinder, L (2000) Introduction: The Context of Evidence-Based Practice, in: Trinder. L and Reynolds, S (eds) *Evidence-Based Practice: A Critical Appraisal.* London: Sage

Vivovskis, M (2002) Missing in Practice? Development and Evaluation at the U.S. Department of Education, in: Mosteller, F and Boruch, R (eds) *Evidence Matters: Randomized Trials in Education Research.* Washington DC: The Brookings Institute

Willinsky, J (2001) The Strategic Education Research Program and the Public Value of Research, in *Educational Researcher* 30(1): 5-14

3

Power, resistance and compliance: teacher education in the universities
a personal recollection

MIKE NEWBY

In this chapter, Mike Newby traces twenty years of government intrusion into UK teacher training, fuelled by a deep suspicion among policy makers of those who have been seen as academic ideologues. He offers an insider view of some of the political shifts described by Stronach and Lather, and sets the context for Avis' analysis of the reformulation of teacher professionalism in chapter five. In contrast with the views of these other authors, however, Newby presents an optimistic view of the potential for educators to influence policy. While he laments the political moves which have eroded professional autonomy, Newby identifies some key ways in which dialogue between educators and policy makers has had positive outcomes.

Things can only get better

I became Chair of the Universities Council for the Education of Teachers (UCET) in 1998, not long after the election triumph in May 1997 of Tony Blair's New Labour government. In a changing world, teacher education stood at a crossroads. Many influential people had questioned whether training teachers was proper work for the universities, some on educational grounds, others for deeper, more ideological reasons. Teacher educators in University Departments of Education (UDEs) and university sector colleges took a different view ....

In January 1992, Kenneth Clarke, Education Minister during Margaret Thatcher's Conservative government, signalled a prominent moment in the recent history of university-based teacher education in England when he called for the location of the training of secondary school teachers to move substantially from the HE campus into the school classroom with 'the school and its teachers ... in the lead in the whole of the training process'(1992: paragraph 22). Twenty-one years later, paragraph 3.25 of the UK Government's 2003 *White Paper* on Higher Education (DfES, 2003) states:

> It is of vital importance that all universities, including leading research universities, continue to regard training for the public services – particularly the training of teachers and health professionals – as a core part of their mission.

What happened to explain the contrast between those two positions?

Experience in England over the last two decades has been of government intervening ever more intrusively into the professional preparation of those who will one day teach. This has prompted a struggle between the universities (embracing their role as academic custodians of the teaching profession, producing new teachers and informing the profession through their research) and the policy makers challenged the right of the universities to maintain this role and even questioned their competence to train practitioners from – as some saw it – their lofty remoteness in the groves of academe. The training of the nation's teachers became the site in which two concepts apparently found themselves opposed: the academic and professional freedoms espoused in Higher Education; and government's determination to raise teacher standards. Mr Clarke proposed that the universities were of but limited importance in achieving the latter. Resulting controls meant a regulatory environment so oppressive that many in the universities seriously questioned whether sustaining a commitment to teacher education was worthwhile.

The CPD contract

Since 1994, the funding of initial teacher education in England, together with its regulation, has been the responsibility of the Teacher Training Agency (TTA). In the winter of 1996-97, the TTA extended this remit to include the funding of school teachers' continuing professional development (CPD) by inviting competitive tenders for a triennium of funding. Forced to bid in a paper-based exercise *for its own on-going work*, half the HE sector failed to secure a contract. This was damaging for many UDEs as well as for the teachers they served. It left large areas of the country without HE-based CPD and seriously threatened the stability of the UDEs, if only because the CPD side of their work was intimately connected to their initial teacher education, usually being staffed by the same people using the same facilities. The results of the bidding exercise suggested that the TTA had little understanding of and even a lack of interest in the way UDEs operated. It also flew in the face of all those who urged the continuity of provision from *initial teacher education*, through *induction*, to *career-long professional development*. It seemed as if the TTA was driving through territory for which it had no map, with a perverse determination to look the other way each time it came to a signpost.

For those working in UDEs, the CPD decision came as the most bizarre of a sequence of measures taken by the TTA since its inception a few years before, all of which seemed designed to emphasise that HE was dispensable in preparing new teachers and developing those already qualified, welcome to bid for work it had always assumed as its own but with every chance that others outside would be preferred. It was evident that, from the time it was established, the TTA unequivocally dominated teacher education (or 'training' as the Agency insisted on calling it) at all its levels. The 1997 CPD bidding decision, for many UDEs a minor catastrophe, marked a low point in the already poor relationship which was building up between the TTA and the HE providers. These were represented by the Universities Council for the Education of Teachers (UCET), an organisation which had begun largely as an academic association but which was increasingly having to re-orientate itself as a lobbying group, seeking to influence policy and often to limit the damage being done to the sector. The CPD decision prompted UCET to make strong representations on behalf of its members and, as a result, a delegation was invited by Estelle Morris, Schools Minister in Tony Blair's New Labour government, to visit her to explain its concerns. Remarkably, such a meeting with a minister had not happened before.

At the meeting, the Minister said she was *unhappy with the way the TTA had handled the CPD bid*. After several years during which the TTA seemed to some to have been waging war on the UDEs, the weight of this statement which could hardly be exaggerated. Could the change of government mean a change of fortune for the UDEs? Might the CPD incident paradoxically mark the beginning of a more constructive period in the development of teacher education in England?

The case against university-based teacher education

It is unlikely that the Agency itself had considered this as a possible consequence of its decision. After all, the TTA had been established if not actually to dismantle the UDEs, at least to limit their influence by imposing its own view of the way in which teachers should be trained. It was not alone. Influential groups and individuals, think-tanks like the *Centre for Policy Studies* and New Right advocates like Chris Woodhead, Her Majesty's Chief Inspector of Schools, were quite open about their wish to prise teacher education away from university control. Under John Major's Conservative administration (1990-97), these people had significant influence. Nearly a year before the Blair government came to power in 1997, the Conservative peer Lord Pearson of Rannoch, in a debate in the House of Lords (*Hansard*, 1996: Vol.573, No.120), described university-based teacher training courses as being controlled by 'a large, powerful, vicious and insular education establishment' and that 'inherent in the activities of these ideologues was the promotion of socialism'. Conceding that 'teacher training is the soil in which the roots of our primary, secondary and indeed university systems feed', he concluded that 'the cancer now runs so deep' that to turn around 'the long march of the institutions ... will be a long and arduous process'. Three years after that Election victory, another influential figure, journalist Melanie Phillips (2002), still felt able to write of 'desperate parents and teachers intimidated by the doctrinaire education orthodoxy'.

Language of 'intimidation', 'cancer' and the 'vicious' education establishment was merely the most incontinent expression of an increasingly popular belief that something was badly amiss in our education service and that the cause could be traced back to the universities. It was not surprising that some would urge that new teachers were not only best trained by teaching real children in real classrooms, overseen by a real teacher, and without all the bogus educational theory with which university lecturers were stuffing their heads, but even that many of the ills of our education system, indeed of our society, could be laid directly at the door of these very academics. Parts of the press demonised 'the Professors of Education' as inveterate complainers, forever calling into question government's attempts to reform education, and even passing on their baseless misgivings to their own students! Eyes rolled to the ceiling at the mere mention of teacher training in the universities.

UCET's remonstrations had not got the universities very far. Until that CPD decision by the Agency, the TTA had carried all before it as it went about changing the system and, regardless of UCET's protests, the sector was largely helpless to resist. In a 1997 press interview, Anthea Millett, first Chief Executive of the TTA, said of the HE providers:

> ... it is crucial not to cut the link between quality and funding. This has been a powerful and effective lever in raising standards, allowing us to reward high-quality providers and show the others that they need to improve. Once you've got them by the finances, their hearts and minds will follow.

Notwithstanding the graceless error in that last assertion (the universities would suggest that she was as mistaken on the question of minds as she certainly was on that of hearts), the ruling philosophy of the Agency was clear enough: link funding to quality, thereby rewarding good performance and punishing bad by taking money (student numbers) away. Since the TTA's inception, and its fruitless urging that a better way to link quality judgments to funding would be to *invest in necessary improvements*, the professional consensus was that the TTA's dealings with sector had been much more stick than carrot. UCET's meeting with the new Minister therefore came at a critical time.

Roots

We must go back a long way to understand why university-based teacher education was held in such low esteem. In 1982, Her Majesty's Inspectors (HMI) produced the first of their reports entitled *The New Teacher in School* (HMI, 1982). In it, they said that a quarter of the people coming out of the teacher training system were ill-prepared. HMI found that student teachers were unimpressed by the theoretical disciplines on which their Education Studies courses were founded, instead craving more of the practical. The word relevance was often heard in those days, meaning *school-based*. Trainee teachers had made clear to HMI their collective theory aversion and their desire for more on the job practical activity.

One consequence of the Report was the establishment in 1984 of CATE, the *Council for the Accreditation of Teacher Education*. CATE determined criteria for courses leading to Qualified Teacher Status (QTS). One of these was that all HE lecturers responsible for training students for classroom practice must themselves have recent and relevant teaching experience at the phase for which their students were preparing. University lecturers were sent off to teach in school classrooms. The question of recent classroom experience would also be asked of applicants interviewed for posts in UDEs, in the search not for bright young academics starting to work their way up the academic ladder but for experienced, credible and high quality school teachers ready to take on the training challenge. For better or worse, that CATE criterion has been influential ever since in the predominance of practitioners over researchers in the UDEs.

CATE's criterion was an attempt to meet the goal of *relevance*. The implication was that people working in UDEs were out of touch. Students demanded lecturers with *classroom credibility* and here was a way of achieving it. However, the 'recent and relevant' principle could be construed as a confession of failure to conceive of the proper sharing of responsibilities, in preparing new teachers, between the schools and UDEs. It implied that, unavoidable though it was to have teachers trained in the HE setting, the worst effects of doing so could in part be mitigated by requiring college lecturers *to be as much like school teachers as possible*. Noone disputed the obvious appropriateness of training new teachers in close contact with real schools and real classrooms, working with real teachers and real pupils. However, CATE had side stepped the deeper question: what could universities offer their student teachers which schools could not, and vice-versa? What should be the proper nature of this partnership? Should HE should do the 'theory' while schools did the 'practice'? CATE failed to formulate a teacher education in which all those helping people learn to become teachers had recent and relevant experience useful to achieving this aim, experience of the kind of work best done in universities, and in the schools, with a good chance the chance that they will be of different and complementary kinds.

In 1990, Sheila Lawlor, in a New Right Centre for Policy Studies pamphlet *Teachers Mistaught: Training theories or Education in Subjects* had no such doubts about the split of responsibilities. For her, Universities should be there to teach intending teachers their subject, schools to teach them how to teach it. She urged the removal from HE of teacher training, with their 'lengthy, doctrinaire and demoralising' courses (1990: 41). The unadorned clarity of her entirely subject-bound view of teacher education – indeed, of school education – was highly influential, perhaps in part because it resonated with the experience at school of those who were at that time running the country: an education in which what was learned were *subjects*.

And so, in January 1992, Education Secretary Kenneth Clarke announced that the *proportion* of training responsibilities would change to become 80% to the schools and 20% to the universities (1992: paragraph 33). The previous September, in an address to the Conservative Party Conference, he had said:

> I meet too many young people who don't go into teaching because they are put off by the length of the course. Or they go on a course and give up because they are put off by the idea of learning too much theory and not enough practice. I want to see students actually getting into a classroom for much more of the time while they train. I want them to learn how to control a noisy class of 30 kids by actually having to do it with the help of an experienced teacher and using their training courses to sort out the problems. (in Furlong *et al.*, 2000:67)

For him, then, this was the nature of teacher training:

- classes are full of noisy kids
- training courses are too long
- courses are there to sort out the problems
- the best help comes from an experienced teacher
- students don't like theory and want more practice

Becoming a teacher was a comparatively uncomplicated thing to do, not far removed from the old canard that 'those who can't do, teach' with its mischievous addition: 'and those who can't teach, teach teachers'.

Clarke's 80/20 split (later it became 60/40, probably when his civil servants realised the difficulties that would ensue were the Minister's words actually to be enforced in practice) made very clear his government's view of the place of HE in the process. However, despite the monochromatic clarity of this prescription and its philosophical flavour, there still remained the problem of actually bringing it about. Was he saying that it should now become the *statutory responsibility* of schools to prepare new teachers? Well, no ... because schools were under no compulsion to do this work if they chose not to. If they did, however, some of the money paid to the universities for teacher training would now have to be forwarded to the schools themselves, where previously they had freely hosted university students. So although schools would apparently *lead* the enterprise, responsibility for managing the finances and for the qualification itself would stay with what might now be termed the *junior partners* – the universities.

Did the schools, however, actually have the facilities such as libraries, and the time to design and deliver teacher education courses in addition to teaching children? The majority made it clear that they didn't see this as their principal task, important and valued though their contribution to it clearly was. It seemed that noone had asked the schools what they thought before advising Mr Clarke. The two HE awards taken by teachers to qualify for QTS (Qualified Teacher Status) were the Bachelor of Education degree (the BEd) and the Postgraduate Certificate in Education (the PGCE). Given that the warrant for these awards resided in the University Senates and Academic Boards, was the Secretary of State really proposing that schools should also have degree awarding powers?

The Department for Education and Science *Circular 9/92* for secondary teacher training (DES, 1992:4, Paragraph 14) spells out the mix of responsibilities (my italics):

> Schools will have a *leading* responsibility for training students to teach their specialist subjects, to assess pupils and to manage classes; and for supervising students and assessing their competence in these respects. HEIs will be responsible for ensuring that courses meet the requirements for academic validation, presenting courses for accreditation, awarding qualifications to successful students, and arranging student placements in more than one school.

The universities, then, were to become little more than accounting centres, school placement offices, and a Senate or Academic Board to approve courses leading to QTS. All the real work was to be done in the schools. Despite talk of partnership, the teaching profession was progressively being disconnected from the universities. The principle which stood in grave danger of being fractured was that which held that our education service was a continuum – from school to university to school: a cycle of learning, teaching and research from which the child would eventually return as the professional to teach others, having been prepared intellectually and practically in the university. Had the 80/20 rule actually come to pass, there would have been very little left in the way of UDEs to be the junior partners of anyone.

Soil

It wasn't entirely surprising that Mr Clarke took the view he did given that he worked in a government driven by what came to be called Thatcherism: a combination of social, political and economic principles which characterised the policies of Margaret Thatcher's term in office. Tenets of Thatcherism included the concept of *enterprise*; of people standing independently 'on their own feet' rather than seeking state support; of the wish to cut taxes by selling off state commitments in the public services and of the consequent move to privatisation. It was anti-monopolist and anti-corporatist, believing that public services would be enhanced by placing them within a market place, establishing league tables of comparative performance, and letting the consumer choose. A school could find itself in direct competition for pupils (and for funding) with neighbouring schools, their one time partners. Directed by locally elected representatives, the Local Education Authorities themselves were targeted, parents being invited, if they wished, to vote for their school to opt out of local control. Teachers, who had been responsible for their pupils' curriculum, found that a new National Curriculum was imposed which took away a key aspect of their professional autonomy.

Underpinning these market place considerations were social, even moral, ones. Britain in the 1970s, prior to Margaret Thatcher's 1979 election victory, was perceived to be in decline. Look, for instance, at its seemingly uncontrollable inflation rate in the late 1970s. Look at the potential, in the consequences of the great oil crises of that decade, for civil unrest. Many perceived their nationhood to be disintegrating as confidence faltered in Britain's status as a Great Power. Who was to blame? Obviously, those who had voted for Mrs Thatcher blamed the previous Labour administration, but others too came in for the same treatment: foreigners (for instance, people in distant places like a country called the 'Pacific Rim', which had the audacity to beat the British in economic performance); trades unions, particularly the coal miners, referred to by Mrs Thatcher as 'the enemy within' (in Collins, 1999); local government, indeed, vested interests wherever they could be found. These included the intellectual élites, sequestered on their university campuses.

It seemed that the educational experiments of the sixties and seventies had failed. The consensus was that a good third or more of pupils left school at sixteen fit for little except the unemployment register. And so we learned to look aghast at our schools, seeing there failure and even teacher militancy: *teachers* – the example-setters to the young – were becoming seditious rabble-rousers, egged on by their unions! The fabric of British society seemed in 1979 to be unravelling, and much of the effort of government during the Thatcher years went into ravelling it up again, albeit to a different weave. In education, when all was done that needed to be done in the schools, it was hardly surprising that the Secretary of State for Education should have announced his intention to reform teacher training in the universities. Here was another monopoly, another group of apparently powerful, unchallenged professionals, intellectuals with vested interests delaying progress. Here was another process which must be exposed to the harsh disciplines of the market place.

Grasping this challenge resonated with a deeper, more pervasive project in England throughout these years: ridding the nation of what Lord Rannoch had called 'socialism'. Mrs Thatcher spoke often about the end of socialism while, in the White House, Ronald Reagan described the Soviets as an 'evil empire' (1983). Those of a similar persuasion in the UK found two educational icons to embody the attitudes they found so reprehensible. One was the modern tendency in the way teachers taught children to read and write (and in particular, the abandonment of *phonics* and *grammar* in favour of 'real books' and the teaching of 'free creative writing'). The second was teacher training in the universities, with its infuriating tendency to want to problematise everything; to see simple acts of teaching as complex psycho-social interventions; to see the raising and schooling of little children as processes in which the child must somehow be placed at the *centre* rather than being firmly told what it must and mustn't do. The universities, it seemed, wanted to meddle, through the preparation of new teachers, in the very limbic systems of society: for example, in the almost febrile interest teacher trainers seemed to show in questions of multicultural education, gender equality and children with special educational needs. If schools were to blame for many of society's ills, then it was the teachers who lay at the heart of the problem, and the virus which had infected them could be found back there, during their training, in the universities.

Mr Clarke strengthened CATE's powers: all the stakeholders in teacher training in different regions were required to collaborate to give the *yea* or *nay* to training courses in their area. The rules said that HE representatives on their CATE committees must be in the minority. Some saw this regionalisation of CATE as a necessary deepening and widening of the powers of government over HE's dominance of teacher training, moving out protectively from the centre of power in London into the regions so that no corner of the land was left unprotected from malign university influence. Another more optimistic view of this extension of CATE's authority was that, for a while at least, teacher educators in universities, their partners in schools, representatives from local government and people from the community all began to work together in considering the development of teacher education in their locality.

Such regional partnerships were never fully developed, however, since CATE was swept away and, in 1994, a new body established in its place by another Conservative Education Minister, John Patten: the Teacher Training Agency.

New growth

For representatives of UCET to be invited in 1997 to meet the Schools Minister, and for her to begin the conversation by saying she was unhappy at what the TTA had done, was a portentous moment. It was essential that the UCET delegation did not squander this opportunity. Courteous, friendly and ready to listen as she was, she was also no doubt thoroughly briefed and (those of us at the meeting assumed) waiting for signs that critics of the universities had been right all along in accusing them of trying to resist reform. The meeting went well and ended with the Minister asking that UCET come to meet her again to see what progress was being made. This was to become the second in a regular series. At last in unpromising circumstances the universities had found the ear of government. TTA's mishandling of the CPD issue had allowed a conversation to begin which began to help inform national policy. The universities were able to demonstrate that, along with the schools and the government with its agencies, they were essential partners in raising the quality and standards of the teaching profession. Furthermore, when they did criticise policy, as they often did, it was from a position of growing trust, rather than one of all too predictable hostility to change of any kind.

Another imperative

In any analysis of this period in the development of teacher education, we cannot ignore the necessities of another market place: that of the teaching profession itself. During the late 1990s, England faced a growing crisis of teacher supply and retention. The constant imposition, both on schools and on UDEs, of what some would say were oppressive regulatory régimes, policed by an ever present and increasingly uncompromising inspectorate, had a negative impact on the readiness of people to enter teaching and of those already in schools to remain as teachers. Arguments about teacher training were always tempered by these facts of life: too much disruption of the system would only exacerbate an already serious problem. To recruit the most gifted people to teaching meant offering them a career which would give free reign to their creativity and autonomy, as well as their wish to help others and to improve society. The joyless necessities of what the training process in the UDEs had become were a poor advertisement for such a future, and many looked elsewhere for career fulfilment. As UCET made this point, it was assisted by the increasingly stark prospects facing government: of schools with no teachers. The TTA, under its second Chief Executive, Ralph Tabberer, prompted by these realities, came to recognise that people cannot perform well if always under threat, and so the relentless drive for higher standards came gradually to be reconciled with the much more subtle quest for higher quality. The result has been that the years between that 1997 meeting and the present have seen a gradual but emphatic change in the context in which people are prepared for teaching which many will claim bodes well for the future.

Conclusion

Discourse, power, resistance – all are words which seem apposite in considering the emergence of HE-based teacher education from its dark winter. Did we in the universities resist? Yes, we resisted the calls to close us down, to eliminate HE from the preparation of succeeding generations of teachers.

Where was the *power*? In No.10 Downing Street, principally, but elsewhere too: education is an important part of the landscape in the public affairs community, and so is fought over by many groups and many individuals, some in the department responsible for Education, some in the TTA, some in the Office for Standards in Education (Ofsted – the inspection service), some in the teaching associations, some in the government think tanks and policy units and some in the profession itself, both in school and university. Higher Education, represented by UCET, was squeezed between them and had to find its own voice in order to emerge as another force to be considered as policy came to be refined, revised or even reversed.

As for *discourse*, my view is that the discourse which UCET had hitherto adopted, perhaps inevitably, given the circumstances, tended to be rebarbative and negative. Later strategy was to change all that and to employ the register we have become familiar with today of collaboration and of collegiality.

Did it work? No – not if you're one of the unregenerate teacher educators of the radical past, passionately claiming the right of the universities to determine their own curricula, their own pedagogical practice, their own intellectual agendas. For them, what's happened has been a massive compromise, with relative peace bought only at the price of near total compliance. But yes, if you believe that the first task in 1997, with the new government waiting to decide on the role of the UDEs in the future of the teaching profession, was survival, and the second was to reclaim at least some professional freedom. So far, at least, nearly all the UDEs have survived. As for freedom, the latest policy coming out of TTA in the form of standards for Qualified Teacher Status (DfES and TTA, 2002) goes further than before to-wards offering back to the HE providers at least some of the autonomy, some of the trust, which they have for so long been denied. The TTA's consultation (TTA, 2003) on how best to link judgements of quality in teacher education and training with the allocation of student numbers and funding is informed by the belief that the current system, which involves Ofsted regularly policing courses and bringing back news of failure to the TTA, with the immediate consequence that the provider loses numbers and so is threatened with closure, has been counter-productive. The TTA has recognised that it can achieve more in the sector if it encourages and supports than if it decries and punishes. This insight presages the start of the next stage in the development of a world class system of teacher education and training in England, one based on a greater measure of trust between academics, their school partners, and the agencies of government than has been the case for twenty years.

References

Clarke, K (1992) *Speech to the North of England Conference.* London: Department for Education and Science

Collins, C (ed) (1999) *Margaret Thatcher: Complete Public Statements 1945–1990* (CD ROM). Oxford: Oxford University Press

Department for Education and Science (1992) *Initial Teacher Training (Secondary Phase)* (Circular 9/92). London: DES

Department for Education and Skills (2003) *The Future of Higher Education.* London: Her Majesty's Stationery Office

Department for Education and Skills and the Teacher Training Agency (2002) *Qualifying to Teach: Professional Standards for Qualified Teacher Status and Requirements for Initial Teacher Training.* London: DfES and TTA

Furlong, J, Barton, L, Miles, S, Whiting, C and Whitty, G (2000) *Teacher Education in Transition: Reforming Professionalism?* Buckingham: Open University Press

Hansard (1996) 573(120) (5 July). London: Her Majesty's Stationery Office

Her Majesty's Inspectorate (1982) *The New Teacher in School.* London: Her Majesty's Stationery Office

Lawlor, S (1990) *Teachers Mistaught: Training in Theories or Education in Subjects?* London: Centre for Policy Studies

Millett, A (1997) Interview in *Times Educational Supplement* (31 January)

Phillips, M (2002) Why I am a Progressive, in *New Statesman* (January)

Reagan, R (1983) Speech to the National Association of Evangelicals (8 March) http://www.presidentreagan.info/speeches/empire.cfm

Teacher Training Agency (2003) *Consultation on the Use of Information about Quality in Allocation Decisions for 2004/05.* London: TTA

PART TWO
CASE STUDIES

4

Contested practices: learning outcomes and disciplinary understandings

SUE CLEGG AND PETER ASHWORTH

Sue Clegg and Peter Ashworth offer a thoughtful analysis of the relatively recent ascendance of the discourse of learning outcomes. This discussion is entwined with those of quality control and audit as determining factors in the development and delivery of curricula, and of the associated contradictions and tensions. The epistemological challenges and assumptions of setting and measuring learning outcomes are discussed, and this discussion is brought alive through the empirical study of the everyday world of academic practitioners, whose evidence reveals the reality of putting learning outcomes policy into practice, as part of a struggle for meaning in both a theoretical and a practical sense.

Introduction

The aim of our paper is to explore the discourse of learning outcomes and to understand how this relatively new methodology for describing curricula is experienced in the everyday world of academic practitioners. In order to achieve this we have adopted the dual strategy of critiquing the socio-political and epistemological basis of learning outcomes, while at the same time analysing in-depth interviews from a small number of academics, in order to understand practise on the ground. The study was not based on a pre-imposed set of dualistic assumptions about the goodness or badness of learning outcomes in relation to other discursive formulations in Higher Education, rather we were open to the discovery of both and mutual dependencies as well as either/or relationships and identities (Hughes, 2002). The empirical data form an exploration of whether and, if so, how particular academics incorporated the new language of learning outcomes into their ways of enacting the routine tasks of devising modules, working out how to deliver them, and setting and marking assessments. The paper, therefore, attempts to go beyond the espoused language of learning outcomes, as they are enshrined in programme and module descriptors, to explore tacit knowledge in the world of practising teachers. The local context of the case study is significant since it was carried out in an institution where the learning outcome approach has been taken very seriously and where course documentation is expressed in a prescribed format. All the participants in the study were therefore practising in a context where learning outcomes were available and communicated to students. Moreover, the learning outcomes approach had been championed by a pro-active team of staff developers, who stressed the belief that the learning outcomes approach gave course teams the scope to clarify and improve their professional practice.

The paper is divided into two parts. In Part One we undertake a critique of the discourse of learning outcomes understood, as 'enacted practices surrounding learning outcomes in contradistinction to the rhetoric' (Avis, 2000:p46). Along with Avis we have emphasised the importance of looking beyond the purely textual formulation of programme specifications (Quality Assurance Agency 2000), to how the national and international contexts define the discursive space of quality assurance (Harvey, 2002). The first part of the paper, therefore, considers the broader socio-political and policy context and contradiction and tensions within quality systems. Arguments about quality are framed within a managerialist discourse of audit, which actively create the organisational environments through its operations (Power 1997). The discourse of quality is not the only one available to academics and we also consider learning outcomes in relation to disciplinary identities. Our argument is not one of incommensurability, but rather that academic identities mean that disciplinarity exists in tension with the language of outcomes. One major assumption of outcomes based learning (OBL) is the notion that learning outcomes can be expressed, albeit imperfectly, and therefore help both students and staff understand what is expected of them. This claim has epistemological dimensions, and we therefore explore the idea of transparency and the extent to which the knowing-how of practice can be made visible. Part Two of the paper deals with the empirical investigation we undertook to extend our knowledge of the ways practitioners think about learning outcomes and how they are understood in relation to the concrete lifeworld of individual practitioners. In this part of the paper we present our methodology and analysis of the data. The categories and understandings of the participants inform our conclusions. The contestation we refer to in the title of the paper is not simply for or against – it involves the struggle for meaning at both theoretical and practical levels.

Part One: Critique
1.1 The socio-political setting

Jackson (2000) argues that the introduction of OBL, of which learning outcomes form a part, came about as part of the shift from elite to mass education. In these newer mass systems quality assurance is part of explicit public policy (Harvey, 2002). These moves are not confined to the UK. The major shake up of Higher Education systems across the globe has involved an alignment of education systems to the needs of the economy (Brown and Lauder, 2001, Brown and Lauder, 1997), and a rejection of the premise that educational professionals can self-regulate and control the quality of what is produced. Jackson (2000) is at pains to argue that the introduction of learning outcomes and OBL is benign and has clear educational advantages. Moreover, given the undoubted movement towards greater control and audit, he argues that the alternative is not a return to an acceptance of professional judgement, characteristic of elite systems, but rather greater control in the form of an imposed common curriculum. In his defence of OBL he argues that the practices and guidance offered by the Quality Assurance Agency, the national regulatory agency for Higher Education in the UK, recognise the need for professional judgement. While the exercise of professional autonomy undoubtedly exists in practice, as Rosie (2002) in his subtle analysis of regulatory discourses in action demonstrates, other commentators have recognised that in the slide to performativity (Barnett, 2000), professional judgement itself is being reorganised.

Jackson (2000) recognises that debates about the learning outcomes approach have become politicised. The linkage of economic competitiveness and the need for Higher Education to deliver multi-skilled flexible workers is a feature of educational reforms internationally (Avis, 2002, Brown and, Lauder, 2001, Clegg, Hudson, and Steel, 2003). Moore (2001) provides an analysis of shifts within the South African Higher Education system, where Higher Education is being reformed as a means of helping to integrate South Africa into the global economy, and in re-balancing the social and economic inequities of the apartheid era. Moore (2001) argues that there has been a shift from a position of 'introjection', where curricula emerged largely as a result of academic influence, to one of 'projection', where curricula are subject to external influence (Barnett, 2000, Moore, 2001). The new language of programme specification as part of the way learning outcomes are expressed is therefore part of these broader restructuring processes. Decisions, which were once under the control of small unscrutinised elites, have moved into the public domain and are subject to external pressure, quality judgements, and regulation. These moves have been analysed as part of a shift from more collegial forms of governance towards managerial control which seeks to align institutions towards the new external imperatives, resulting in what Henkel (2000) describes as considerable 'organisational ambiguity' (p54).

There are also tensions within the idea of learning outcomes itself. Avis (2000) points out that learning outcomes have multiple discursive locations. The move towards greater transparency is linked to two very different traditions. The first is allied to competence-based programmes where outcomes are clearly defined and are based mainly on practical accomplishments. The second is rooted in critique of educational practice and based on trying to make curricula more transparent to non-traditional learners. This second tradition rests on a critique of the introverted practices of academy, which were based on the shared social and cultural capital of academics and the students they taught, and the reproduction of certain kinds of mastery (Bourdieu, 1990). Advocates of widening participation and expansion of higher education, therefore, argued that OBL was a way of making more visible to students what they were to achieve, thus shifting the focus from the teachers' knowledge towards the student as a learner.

While recognising the duality of the debates about learning outcomes Avis (2000) argues the need to analyse 'enacted practices' (p46). He points to the danger of technicised process, and the way in which the textual practices of learning outcomes produce 'readerly' texts which limit the scope for agency on the part of students and staff. These readerly texts are part of a prescribed language of audit, review and evaluation based on common templates. In contrast 'writerly' texts invite the reader to write themselves in, but despite the rhetoric of student control of their own learning, the texts available to students rarely allow them to write themselves in. The potentially emancipatory effects of allowing students access to understanding the processes whereby they can achieve their goals is already delimited by the policy imperatives described above.

Learning outcomes and programme specification may appear as neutral and useful instruments of pedagogic improvement. They no doubt challenge academics to think more publicly and rigorously about the outcomes of student learning. However, it would be disingenuous to dismiss the ways in which OBL is part of a broader discursive turn. Jackson argues that the considerable dissent is 'not fundamentally against the approach but is concerned with the bureaucracy that OBL demands in order to demonstrate the connections between outcomes and learning and assessment process' (Jackson, 2000:p136). However, the form of his argument is positivist, presenting us with a neutral technique (OBL) which exists independently of its discursive location. Our argument is not a simple for or against, it is an attempt to understand what learning outcomes mean. In the next section we look at how these newer discourses of OBL interconnect with traditional academic orderings, based on the idea of disciplines.

1.2 Disciplinarity and academic identities

Henkle (2000) is one of the many authors pointing to the critical role disciplinary practices play in sustaining academic identities, which she locates in the interplay between disciplinarity and organisation. Disciplines frame what it is to be an academic and while the idea of disciplinary communities elides differences between members, discipline as a set of elaborate discursive practices remains important. Disciplinarity has also been at the heart of the meaning of studentship. Barnett (2003), and Edwards and Usher (2000), have noted a shift from studentship defined as one who studies texts, to the idea of lifelong learner preoccupied with the creation of a self. Edwards and Usher (2000) base their analysis on an argument about the globalisation and the time space compression implied by the adoption of new technologies and the threats to discipline boundaries new forms of knowledge entail. While there is an element of exaggeration in their arguments, there are now multiple sources of knowledge and legitimation (Gibbons, 1999). Disciplines by their very nature have internal and well understood models for validating knowledge produced inside the discourse, whereas the newer discourses suggested by Gibbons (1999) lack this framing and, according to him, depend on enhanced social accountability and broadly based systems of quality control. This chimes with the themes in the previous section, when instead of autonomous professional judgement, these newer discourses depend on more customer orientated judgements. These judgements are not necessarily at odds with disciplinary knowledge but they do represent a re-ordering.

It could be argued that learning outcomes are entirely compatible with discipline knowledge and do not present a threat to disciplinary identities. Indeed this is what Jackson (2000) claims. However, this ignores the ways in which the discourses are themselves productive. The production of subject templates tells us little about the sorts of texts being produced, and whether they are readerly or writerly in the ways Avis suggests. The processes that Rosie (2002) describes suggest that academics struggle to make them writerly texts by emphasising that the descriptions themselves cannot capture the complexities of the processes in the classroom (Hussey and Smith, 2003). If the advocates of OBL achieve their aim of a clearer focus on the student's learning, one would expect to see transformations in academics' relationship to their own practice, so that alongside thinking about the curriculum from the perspective of disciplinary knowledge, they would think from a pedagogical stance. One of our reasons for engaging in empirical work was to see if we could understand how this was happening in practice.

There is evidence from other literature (Becher, 1989, Kogan, 2000, Neumann, Parry, and Becher, 2002) that the preservation of disciplinarity remains strong, and is heavily rewarded in other aspects of academic life, especially in research. While outcomes, of themselves, do not undermine disciplinarity, thinking from pedagogy may shift the ways disciplinarity is understood. Moore argues, following on a suggestion of Bernstein that:

> ... for an integrated-type model to establish itself, the conditions have to be created in which a community of academics united in a common project, can come to agreement on what is to count as valid knowledge, why, and how it is to be recognised in the context of that programme: in other words, to arrive at a social episte-mology of curriculum which provides the basis for continuing col-lective practice over time, and for a stable and sustainable academic identity. (Moore, 2001:p16)

The epistemological basis for thinking about new curricula, based on learning outcomes, forms the basis for the next section.

1.3 Transparency and epistemological limits

If learning outcomes and OBL are operationalised, it requires academics to model the linkages between what is to be learned, the educational process, and what is actually learned (Jackson, 2000). This practice 'draws upon notions of visibility, transparency and audit as well as clearly defined learning outcomes' (Avis, 2000.p41-42). The prevalence of metaphors of transparency has been described by Strathern (2000) in her paper on 'The Tyranny of Transparency', where she shows that transparency, rather than being neutral and obvious, has a tyrannous dimension, as we suggested in Section 1.1., and operates so that other kinds of reality are 'knowingly eclipsed' (Srathern, 2000:p309). Transparency metaphors rest on positivist assumptions that there is an unmediated real which can be perceived. These positivist assumptions imply that with the right support, and intellectual effort, the practical wisdom of practitioners can be made visible through learning outcomes which are intelligible to staff and students alike. However, Hussey and Smith (2002) argue that there is a fundamental epistemological confusion here. Based on the Rylian distinction between knowing-that and knowing-how, they argue that the attempt to specify learning outcomes involves a process of trans-lating the knowledge-how of professional practice into knowledge-that type statements. This practice ignores the gap between the two types of knowing and is in their view either fatuous or impossible. Statements can and are of course being produced, but they do not carry meaning without recourse to the knowing-how. For students this is recursive, since if meaning is dependent on knowing-how they would already have had to acquire significant meta-cognitive under-standing of their own learning processes in the particular cognitive domain. *Progress Files* (Clegg, 2003) represent the procedural but not the epistemological ground for supposing that students can and do engage in this way.

Parallel epistemological arguments have been made in relation to re-flective practice. Tomlinson (Tomlinson, 1999a, Tomlinson, 1999b), like Hussey and Smith (2002), argues that the Rylian knowing-how may be entirely tacit. People may not be able to tell. They certainly are unlikely to be able to tell in the sorts of procedural language of learn-ing outcomes. Many experiments with different forms of self-aware poetic writing are attempts to grapple with a language for reflective practice that does not rest on simplistic realist assumptions (Bleakley, 2000). Academics as scholars in the humanities and social sciences have been grappling with issues of representation and epistemology for centuries, yet in their pedagogical practice they are being invited to set aside these concerns and operate within crude positivist formu-lations based on ideas of transparency. Bleakley (2000, 1999) has warned of the dangers for pedagogic innovation if analyses of educa-tional processes are not as rigorous as those expected in other subject areas, yet academic developers could be accused of taking this risk in championing overly simplistic versions of OBL.

This might be speculative, were it not for the ways discourses are pro-ductive as described above, and the way audit produces organisa-tional forms. However, what was striking to us when we searched the literature was that there was relatively little detailed evidence, as op-posed to broad brush reconstructions by proponents of the approach (Watson, 2002) of whether and how academics use learning outcomes in their routine practice. Critique by its nature is immanent, and ex-plores possibilities that may not transpire in everyday practice. Avis (2000) adopts the strategy of working with ideal types to push some of his theoretical speculations to their limits. We think this is useful and have followed him in these introductory remarks. We now turn to our investigation, not to prove or disprove any of the above, but to continue the interrogation and to attempt to discover other possible subject positions which were not evident to us through deconstructive logic alone.

Part Two: The Study

The design of the study emerged from extended discussions with a group of colleagues, who came together in order to explore research methodology, with the aim of sharing our learning through the investigation of a mutually agreed topic.[1] The group were all interested in Higher Education research and included people with backgrounds in linguistics, computer science, politics, nursing, sociology psychology and art. Two of the group were working in the University Registry, the others were practising teachers or researchers. The idea of investigating learning outcomes came out of an exploration of our disciplinary orientations and a growing awareness that we were using different language and framing to explore common phenomena. The colleagues from Registry had observed that these differences were reflected in how validation documentation was put together and the perceived ease or difficulty of different subject groups in describing their learning outcomes. The final documentation itself appeared to reflect these differences of style: the computer scientists, for example, produced very precise and detailed maps of learning outcomes.[2] We became very interested, therefore, in the sorts of language individual academics used to express their thought processes as they designed, delivered and assessed modules. We worked from within a broadly phenomenological approach, aiming to bracket our presuppositions, and paying detailed attention to the individual's own framing (Ashworth, 1999, Ashworth and Lucas, 2000). Most of the literature review and formal theoretical thinking came out of our engagement with the empirical data, not prior to it, beyond satisfying ourselves that there did not appear to be anything in the existing literature that had explored the topic in the way we proposed.

We chose to collect data by interviewing a small number of colleagues (ten in all) from a range of disciplinary backgrounds. The interviews were planned in some detail as a number of different interviewers were involved. As our intention was to look at how professionals think about practice, we chose to focus on the module rather than course level. We approached the interview by asking respondents to choose a particular module and talk through in detail how they designed and planned it, how they put together the assessments and explained the assessments to the students and how they marked pieces of work. We also asked them what gave them most pleasure in a piece of work and how they knew when it had gone wrong. We asked them about things they valued but did not assess, and whether they had ideas about what a good practitioner in the discipline was like. We only probed directly about whether they used learning outcomes at the end of the interview, as we were interested in their framing rather than conformity with the official discourse.

2.1 Analysis

Our approach resulted in a density of material relating to how individuals approached the design and delivery of their modules. Respondents' own understanding of the context of practice shaped how they thought about learning outcomes. The institutional setting for learning outcomes was a constant where all students are given learning outcomes for their course as a matter of policy, but how respondents reacted was highly variable. For example, interviewee A highlighted issues such as the expertise of staff, the weighting of content through decisions about the allocation of time, and the availability of materials for private study, rather than learning outcomes in the design of a module. In contrast, for interviewee E learning outcomes were problematical because they did not recognise student characteristics and variety. Interviewee C was a very experienced computer analyst and gave a detailed description of his approach, using real life examples. Whereas usually the direction of planning is presumed to be from learning outcomes to the design of the learning experiences, this respondent drew on a large pool of possible Problem Based Learning experiences as a starting point. He then used these as a way of deciding how to fulfil learning outcomes. He argued that in practice the mapping was obvious, but that since the learning outcomes are a kind of contract with the students, as they themselves have been told, it would have been serious if such a mapping had not been found.

> We did feel it was important that they had problem based learning here, that there was a real live problem for them to solve. Both x and I who were involved have both got real life experience of thousands of problems so it was almost the wrong way round. It was almost here's a problem, now how do we map that back to the learning objectives? Now it just so happened that it was such a rich problem area that that mapping was relatively straightforward. What our approach would have been if we hadn't found the

> mapping area I don't know because as I said to the students the learning objectives are the contract really. (Interviewee C)

This tutor was skilled at finding material which could meet the contractual framework set by giving the students the learning outcomes for the course. However, he was not the only respondent to point to the contractual nature of the student relationship. Interviewee E also indicated that learning outcomes are a basis for designing student assessment because of the way they are presented to students, but he regretted the nature of goal-orientation of assessment in place of the educational purpose of assessment in gauging general understanding.

The type of student is significant. Interviewee C was teaching mature professionals and official learning 'objectives' sometimes went by the board. He used them as a kind of checklist, but reflected on the dangers of inflexibility, given that the *raison d'être* of his course is responsiveness to the industrial/professional needs of the students and the commercial partners.

> The learning objectives are fine at the level they are at but they are only objectives aren't they and they break down ...You are aware that in this particular case one of the drivers has got to be what does industry want out of the people out there which makes it slightly different I guess – in partnership that they helped us put the course together. (Interviewee C)

Students and their relationship to the outside profession are the critical factor for him in structuring his pedagogical thinking.

In contrast, for interviewee J, a bio-medical science specialist, subject knowledge was the overriding driver. She expressed frustration at the way learning outcomes appeared bureaucratic rather than knowledge related, after acknowledging the usefulness of simple outcomes:

> Sometimes you are criticised very strongly at validation events about the learning outcomes ... And I don't think that that is helpful to anybody in designing units at all. I think they're helpful in enabling lecturers to think about things [the skills] that are being developed [in students]. But by putting constraints on us, in the wording that we use for them and the fact that they want you to put in so many things that are not, that are skills related... as opposed to knowledge related and what they do does not help in us trying to communicate to students what we expect that student to

get at the Yes... Yeah, I mean what annoys a lot of people is that the 'Indicative Content' comes last on all of these things! (points to unit document). Whereas WE think that this is the most important thing! (bangs on the 'Indicative Content' section with hand repeatedly) That's where we start! That's where every scientists starts! You know, some people... you know become educationalised and things and you know, they can see it from the other point of view. But the majority of people start here (points to section) And that's the last thing on the unit descriptor! (Interviewee J)

The tension between learning outcomes and disciplinary frameworks, which we highlighted in our theoretical discussion, came out in a number of other interviews. All these tutors were struggling with the issues, rather than simply rejecting the learning outcomes or retreating into cynicism. For example, interviewee G was a new lecturer working in social policy. For him, specific contingencies to do with a module in which interdisciplinary team teaching was prominent raised numerous pedagogical issues. The elements of the module were well-specified in terms of learning outcomes, but the transparency these offered to the students did not touch on the major communication issues: how to engage the students with the theoretical underpinnings of the social policy material, and how to encourage students to take an in-depth interest in the material (Drew, 1998). The use of portfolios as a means of student development and assessment was clearly related to a number of specific and generic learning outcomes, which were communicated to students, but the actualisation of these abstract descriptions was a matter of ongoing negotiation and repeated module planning. In sum, learning outcomes were implicated in the experience of this module but played a minor role in the formation of the innovative pedagogy.

The intellectual difficulty of relating learning outcomes to the complexities of both subject knowing and understanding of students' aspirations and orientations, relates directly to the epistemological issues we discussed before. Throughout the interviews there is a sense of gaps, of where the language of description is inadequate to the complexities of practice and feeling. In the descriptions of good assignments tutors often reached for the intangibles. The quotes below are from a fine artist and a biomedical scientist:

> I think seeing them sort of lift off sort of thing so they have had a set of experiences and they have made it part of their world (Interview Eight)

> Yea, seeing them grow, yeah. But I also get satisfaction when the students get a very lovely mark in the exams (Interviewee J)

Across the interviews, when discussing marking assignments there was a sense that tutors knew what good work looked like: they formed holistic impressions:

> Right. I have the [marking] grid in front of me. The grid isn't the model answer kind so it isn't the case of going through and ticking every good point. It is a case of reading the material that they have got. I don't know whether I'm allowed to say this but there is certainly an element of gut feeling at the end of having read. I'm probably a top down sort of a person. I probably get a feel that this is a 55 and then justify that in the marking grid... If the gut feeling still says 55 then you justify it. And then you must bring the moderating process in because I feel sort of OK doing that but then again knowing the people you are working with is quite useful. OK because I know that the guy that is going to be doing the moderating is quite the opposite so I know that I am going to be checked by a bottom up person so I feel comfortable. I wouldn't be quite so comfortable if I didn't know that there was that sort of approach coming. (Interviewee C)

A number of aspects appear important, the 'gut' feeling based on tacit knowledge, the transgressive tone, which suggests that this sort of judgement no longer carries legitimacy, and a recognition that checking by other professionals is important, rather than the marking grid as such. The relationship of assessment to learning outcomes depends on tacit knowledge and some of that necessary imprecision is also part of the process of communicating with the students:

> Well the first thing they get in all the units as a standard is the marking scheme so they know what they are aiming for. Some of the marking grids are a bit woolly so they need explaining. Woolliness is the negative way of looking at you can be creative here. And certainly the one that I am talking about is a bit woolly for the very reason that we wanted them to be able to take themselves off wherever they wanted to. (Interviewee C)

Fuzziness in relation to learning outcomes appears well understood on the ground. However, as interviewee J complained, this is not reflected in the meta-language of validation.

Concluding thoughts

Our final remarks are more a form of reflection rather than a conclusion. The paper has pointed to the *aporias* of thinking in relationship to the discourse of learning outcomes. How significant these gaps are in practice depends on context. We have seen the richly complex insights our respondents brought to their thinking about teaching, based on knowledge of their students, their discipline, their values, and the emotional experience of pleasure at the 'lovely mark', 'the lift off'. Learning outcomes can be seen as a way of checking back on professional judgements which have been already formed, or as one way of framing discussion about pedagogic innovation in course teams. They certainly seem to be a fact of life. However, none of the respondents spontaneously used the language of learning outcomes to describe their thinking processes. We had ample evidence of creative pedagogical thought in our interviews, which is one of the aims of the OBL movement. However, it must be questioned whether the formal apparatus constructed by the Quality Assurance Agency and formal internal procedures supports or undermines these achievements. The bureaucratisation of Higher Education is an accomplished fact, but we must surely be drawing on research to argue that it is process, not regulation, that can bring lasting improvements for students (Hussey and Smith, 2003). The danger is that in formulating the student experience around a contract based on learning outcomes, ideas of discipline, professional judgement and studentship are distorted.

Notes

1   Our thanks go to Alexa Christou, Janet Hargreaves, Christine O'Leary, John Rowe, John Steel, Stephen Wan.

2   The composition of the group undoubtedly affected our metaphors for thinking about the problem and in particular ideas of translation and moving from one language to another which were common experiences for both the linguist and the computer scientists.

References

Ashworth, P (1999) 'Bracketing' in phenomenology: Renouncing assumptions in hearing about student cheating, in *International Journal of Qualitative Studies in Education*, 12(6): 707-712

Ashworth, P and Lucas, U (2000) Achieving empathy and engagement: a practical approach to the design, conduct and reporting of phenomenographic research, in *Studies in Higher Education*, 25(3): 295-308

Avis, J (2000) Policing the subject: Learning outcomes, managerialism and research in PCET, in *British Journal of Educational Studies*, 48(1): 38-57

Avis, J (2002) Social capital, collective intelligence and expansive learning: Thinking through the connections. Education and the economy, in *British Journal of Educational Studies*, 50(3): 308-326

Barnett, R (2000) Supercomplexity and the curriculum, in *Studies in Higher Education*, 25(3): 255-265

Barnett, R (2003) *Beyond All Reason.* Buckingham: Society of Research into Higher Education and Open University Press

Becher, T (1989) *Academic Tribes and Territories: Intellectual enquiry and the cultures of disciplines.* Milton Keynes: Society of Research into Higher Education and Open University Press

Bleakley, A (1999) From reflective practice to holistic reflexivity, in *Studies in Higher Education*, 24(3): 315-330

Bleakley, A (2000) Writing with invisible ink: Narrative confessionalism and reflective practice, in *Reflective Practice*, 1(1): 11-24

Bourdieu, P (1990) *Homo Academicus.* Cambridge: Polity

Brown, P and Lauder, H (2001) *Capitalism and Social Progress: The future of society in a global economy.* Basingstone: Palgrave

Brown, P and Lauder, H (1997) Education, globalisation and economic development, in: Halsey, A H *et al.* (eds) *Education, Culture, Economy, Society.* Oxford: Oxford University Press

Clegg, S (2003) Critical reading: Progress files and the production of the autonomous learner, 11th Improving Student Learning Conference, Hinkley: 1-3 September

Clegg, S, Hudson, A and Steel, J (2003) The emperor's new clothes: Globalisation and e-learning, in *British Journal of Sociology of Education*, 24(1): 40-53

Drew, S (1998) Students' perceptions of their learning outcome, in *Teaching in Higher Education*, 3(2): 197-217

Edwards, E and Usher, R (2000) *Globalisation and Pedagogy: Space, place and identity.* London:Routledge

Gibbons, M (1999) Changing research practices, in: Brennan, J *et al* (eds) *What Kind of University? International perspectives on knowledge, participation and governance.* Milton Keynes: Society for Research into Higher Education and Open University Press

Harvey, L (2002) Evaluation for what?, in *Teaching in Higher Education*, 7(3): 245-263

Henkel, M (2000) *Academic Identities and Policy Change in Higher Education.* London: Jessica Kingsley

Hughes, C (2002) Beyond the poststructuralist-modern impasse: The woman returner as 'exile' and 'nomad', in *Gender and Education*, 14(4): 411-424

Hussey, T and Smith, P (2002) The trouble with learning outcomes, *Active Learning in Higher Education*, 3(3): 220-233

Hussey, T and Smith, P (2003) The use of learning outcomes, in *Teaching in Higher Education*, 8(3): 357-368

Jackson, N (2000) Programme specification and its role in promoting an outcomes model of learning, in *Active Learning in Higher Education*, 1(2): 132-151

Kogan, M (2000) Higher education communities and academic identity, in *Higher Education Quarterly*, 54(3): 207-216

Moore, R (2001) Policy-driven curriculum restructuring: Academic identities in transition? [online] Higher Education Close Up. Conference available from: www.leeds.ac.uk/edcol/documents/00001803.htm [Accessed April 2003]

Neumann, R, Parry, S and Becher, T (2002) Teaching and learning in their disciplinary contexts: A conceptual analysis, in *Studies in Higher Education*, 27(4): 405-417

Power, M (1997) *The Audit Society: Rituals of verification.* Oxford: Oxford University Press

Quality Assurance Agency (2000) Guidelines for Preparing Programme Specifications. [online]. Available from: http://www.qaa.ac.uk/crntwork/progspec/contents.htm [Accessed 05/03/03] .

Rosie, A (2002) The undergraduate social science curriculum and its location: regulatory discourses in action, in: Jary, D (ed) *Benchmarking and Quality Management: The debate in UK higher education.* Birmingham: C-SAP

Schön, D (1983) *The Reflective Practitioner.* New York: Basic Books

Schön, D (1987) *Educating the Reflective Practitioner.* San Francisco: Jossey-Bass

Strathern, M (2000) The tyranny of transparency, in *British Educational Research Journal*, 26(3): 309-321

Tomlinson, P (1999a) Conscious reflection and implicit learning in teacher preparation. Part 1: Recent light on an old issue, in *Oxford Review of Education*, 25(3): 405-424

Tomlinson, P (1999b) Conscious reflection and implicit learning in teacher preparation. Part II: Implications for a balanced approach, in *Oxford Review of Education*, 25(4): 533-544

Watson, P (2002) The role and integration of learning outcomes into the educational process, in *Active Learning in Higher Education*, 3(3): 203-219

5

Re-thinking trust in a performative culture: the case of post-compulsory education

JAMES AVIS

James Avis returns to the issue of government surveillance and control of education addressed in Part 1, looking at the teaching profession in the context of contemporary understandings of work relations in the United Kingdom. He argues for the re-forming of teacher professionalism to accord with the conditions of risk and uncertainty that have led, in other areas of employment, to a new emphasis on trust. Ironically, the high risk conditions in which contemporary education is undertaken are accompanied, he argues, by the erosion of trust: teachers are subjected to the relentless monitoring and regulation of their performance by government agencies against criteria imposed from outside the profession.

This chapter explores teacher professionalism in the post-compulsory sector. To contextualise this it is necessary to discuss globalisation, competitiveness and allied notions related to performativity, managerialism as well as the English route to socio-economic modernisation.

Competitiveness Settlement

It is has become almost a cliché to talk of an educational settlement formed around post-compulsory education. Settlement is used here to refer to a generally agreed framework or set of assumptions surrounding post-compulsory education and training and its relation to the economy (see Avis, 1993; Avis *et al*, 1996). Settlements seek to bring together a range of constituents, from educationalists to industrialists, as well as attempting to take on board the interests of ordinary people and their children. This section begins with an examination of reflexive modernisation. This understanding of contemporary western society aligns with an interpretation of the knowledge economy and globalisation, sitting alongside a particular understanding of the economy and the role of education in preparing young people for work.

Reflexive Modernisation

For Beck (1992) and Giddens (1998) simple modernity, characterised by industrialisation, has run its course. At its apogee the Keynesian welfare state promised full employment and a variety of supportive social structures. Other characteristics were mass production and consumption, which enabled full employment in semi-skilled and unskilled manufacturing occupations. These Fordist relations have been undermined by globalisation and the response has been the call for post-Fordist work patterns, utilising high skill and high trust relations to produce value added products. The move towards reflexive modernisation and its embodiment in the risk society provides a terrain in which a new political and economic context is forged. Previous certainties give way to questioning uncertainty and the challenging of old orthodoxies. Beck (1992) has described the risk society as characterised by manufactured uncertainty which undermines expert and scientific knowledge. The way in which this can be resolved is through debate located within a democratic politics, the outcome of which will determine the resulting strategy: risk becomes democratised. This provides a basis for a reflexive modernity which examines self-critically the potential consequences of its actions. There is a link between these notions and the wider development of trust relations. Such a conceptualisation leads to a re-thinking of the nature of teacher professionalism and brings with it the potential for questioning the teaching profession's own knowledge base.

Competitiveness

Reflexive modernisation underlies the competitiveness settlement which emphasises the development of a high skills, knowledge based economy in which work is marked by high levels of trust and creativity. One would imagine teachers' work being marked by such relations, as it is construed as pivotal in developing those entering the knowledge economy. It is taken for granted that education has an important role to play in contributing to national competitiveness. Such an educational settlement has been accomplished and is one that traverses political parties (DfEE, 1996). Smith (1994), writing in relation to hegemony, illustrates the way in which the current educational settlement disarms critique. Whilst education's role within competitiveness can be questioned, this remains the terrain within which it is situated.

High Skills

In the competitiveness settlement the ready association between the pursuit of competitiveness and the development of a high skills economy needs examination. These ideas could be transferred to education, suggesting that high skill, high trust relations could set the context in which innovatory educational practices are developed. After all, education is charged with developing the knowledge workers of the future. In this case education plays a key role in developing the human, and in some cases, social capital required by the economy. The former refers to the individual's expertise, skills and knowledge, whereas the latter refers to the social networks and patterns of trust relations within which the individual is located (see Baron *et al*, 2001). The need to develop social capital is in part reflected by the increasing emphasis placed in education upon the development of key skills or those related to enterprise, both of which carry a significant social weight. This can be seen in the high levels of social skill associated with problem solving, team work or indeed creativity, and the resulting social skills whose development is thought to contribute towards economic competitiveness (see for example, Brown, Green, Lauder, 2001; DfES, 2001, p2).

It is important to qualify the ready association of high skills with competitiveness. Keep (1997, 1999) and others have suggested that there are a number of routes that can be pursued to achieve this goal, some but not all of which will be based on a high skills strategy (Brown, 2001). Brown *et al* (2001) draw attention to the peculiarities of the English route to competitiveness in that the economy is polarised into high and low skill sections, suggesting the high skill route is to be preferred, as it can deliver greater social and economic benefits for all. However, the rhetorical celebration and acceptance of the high skills trajectory is undermined by the reality of the English economy, in which low skills remains a significant route to profitability. This has resulted in a relatively low waged economy where competition on price rather than quality is a feature of mass markets and undermines the development of a high skills economy (Hutton, 1995; Lauder, 2001).

For Brown *et al* the pursuit of the high skills route entails intervention into the labour market, so that low waged, low skill employment becomes unviable and employers find it necessary to invest in the skills of their workforce. There would then be an economic imperative for employers to move in the direction of high skilled labour, leading to increased wages and competition based on quality rather than price, which would itself encourage further investment in workforce skills.

New Labour's strategy is contradictory in that alongside a commitment to the development of a high skills economy rests an interest in sustaining flexible labour markets, able to attract inward investment (see Blair, 2001). Flexible labour markets are thought to sustain relatively high levels of employment and to sit closely with a concern to break dependency cultures through welfare-to-work strategies which re-moralise the poor and encourage the development of a culture of 'rights and responsibilities', based on 'something for something'. Inward investment can generate higher levels of employment but, is more often than not based on low level skills which contribute to the development of a low waged/low skilled economy in which competition is based on price (Brown *et al*, 2001). New Labour's strategy is two fold. Firstly, through the development of flexible labour markets it encourages demand for labour. Secondly, education is to develop the human and social capital required for a high skills economy. The (unsupported) idea is that a pool of highly skilled and employable workers will encourage employers to make use of such a resource (see for example Brown *et al*, 2001).

Social Inclusion and Cohesion
New Labour claims that a society which offers employment in flexible labour markets can, at the same time, secure a culture of learning that encourages people to invest in their own development: a culture in

which competitiveness will be attained and social cohesion developed (DfES, 2001). It is unlikely that such a strategy, working within the current parameters of the English economy, will succeed (Crouch, Finegold, Sako, 1999). This economy is characterised by a polarisation between a high skilled segment of the economy and a significantly large low skilled sector. New Labour's strategy does very little to interrupt the relationship between low wages and competition based on price, which needs to be transformed if the high skills route is to be embraced throughout the economy.

Trust

The competitiveness settlement embodies a specific understanding of work relations, as well as a particular model of the economy. A high skills economy is inextricably tied to high wages and high trust work relations. Workers, through the exercise of skills and knowledge, create value added products, and the acquisition and manipulation of knowledge becomes pivotal to attaining competitive advantage. It is through the continuous exercise of a range of transferable and intellectual skills that the worker will be enabled to keep pace with the rapidity of social and economic change (Young, 1998). It is here that the skills associated with the symbolic analyst come into play and where creativity emerges (Reich, 1991). Working conditions marked by hierarchical relations fail to generate work based cultures that lend themselves to creative endeavour, whereas team work, collective problem solving and non-hierarchical relations draw on the intellectual skills of the worker. To facilitate such a process, relationships based on trust and risk taking need to be established, freeing the worker to express creativity and contribute towards collective problem solving. Trust becomes a prerequisite for the knowledge worker: without it risks will not be taken and new ideas will remain unexpressed, hindering competitiveness as well as processes of continuous improvement. These approaches are transferable to education since the education system is charged with developing future knowledge workers. The implication is that high skill, high trust relations in education can set the context in which innovatory practices develop. Such arguments suggest the need to develop a re-formed teacher professionalism, one that accords with the new conditions of risk and uncertainty.

This argument has drawn out the contradictions surrounding the competitiveness settlement. There is an unevenness within the English economy, where alongside a high skills sector exists a significant low skills one, marked by low trust employment relations which have more in common with Fordism than the creative and democratic work relations promised by reflexive modernisation. There are a number of ways in which we can respond to these arguments. Reflexive modernisation and its appropriation by New Labour can be viewed as glossing over capitalist relations that seek to deepen the exploitation of wage labour and reduce expenditure on the welfare state. Callinicos (2001) makes such a point in his critique of Gidden's third way politics, which is seen as being predicated on neo-liberalism. Alternatively, reflexive modernisation can be viewed as a description of the socio-economic and political context in which teachers labour. Its conceptualisation of risk and uncertainty, as well as the vulnerability of expert knowledge, is relevant here, as is the re-cognition of the feeling of insecurity that characterises much employment where restructuring has become commonplace (Bourdieu, 1998; Callinicos, 1999).

The notions of risk, uncertainty, insecurity and the vulnerability of expert knowledge can also be invoked in the struggle to redefine and develop progressive forms of professionalism, which transcend the limitations of legitimated teacher professionalism, which are characteristic of the social democratic settlement (Grace, 1987; Lawn, 1988, 1996). In this case teachers were granted autonomy within the classroom as curricular and pedagogic experts. The assault of the new right over the last thirty years, together with sensibilities derived from reflexive modernisation, has undermined this form of professionalism.

Performativity

It is a paradox that teachers' work relations and allied constructions of professionalism seem nearer to Fordism than to the professionalism implied within reflexive modernisation (Codd, 1999). This is best illustrated in the emphasis placed upon performance management and its resonance with Fordist work relations, as well as the ongoing attempt to control the work force, all of which seem out of kilter with understandings of the knowledge economy (Morris, 2001).

Such practices crisscross the state education system from schools and colleges to universities (Nixon and Ranson, 1997). For example, the Learning and Skills Council (LSC) which is responsible for post-compulsory education and training in England describes its mission; 'to raise participation and attainment through high-quality education and training which puts *the learner first*' [my emphasis] (2001, unnumbered). Such a vision is consistent with a system of accountability based upon performance management and continuous improvement. The parameters of these performative practices are well known and involve target setting, action planning and the development of performance indicators that are used to measure successful outcomes. These practices are set within the context of a contract which determines the overarching targets and outputs to be attained (see Husbands, 2001). These targets and performance indicators finally confront the classroom teacher, defining the context within which practitioners operate, commonly monitored through staff appraisal. Although these performative practices set context within which teachers labour, they are subject to appropriation and mediation as they pass through institutional levels. Nevertheless, they have determinate effects in that whilst appropriation and mediation may be manifestations of resistance, accommodation, or even survival strategies, the overarching targets have to be addressed. In post-compulsory education and training the Teachers Pay Initiative (TPI), which is akin to the threshold payments used in schools, serves to deepen these processes and provides a clearer specification of what it is to be a teacher or lecturer and the expectations associated with that role. Allied to this is the promise that teachers and institutions attaining their targets will be rewarded by light touch inspections, the reduction of bureaucracy and greater institutional autonomy (see Nash, 2001; Morris, 2001). Concurrently, there is the threat that under-performance will be subject to close scrutiny with the eventual withdrawal of funding.

As a case in point it is useful to examine self-assessment and inspection régimes in the Learning Skills Sector as well as the TPI. In its overview of post-16 quality improvement the DfEE provides a rationale for a culture of continuous improvement. Providers of post-16 learning are to ensure that:

- all learners achieve excellence through learning

- they facilitate teaching and learning excellence

- learning represents value for money

- learning meets the needs of learners, employers and the local community and benefits the economy as a whole. (DfEE, 2001a, p2)

The case for continuous improvement is focused on the development of learners, with teachers and teaching placed in a subordinate position. Teaching is seen to facilitate learning: the learners' needs are paramount. This view matches the now dominant notion that learners and their employers/sponsors can articulate learners' needs and that if these are not adequately addressed, providers should be held accountable (Hall, 2001).

In the DfEE rationale for continuous improvement there is a concern to colonise teachers' subjectivity. Staff should be 'committed to the pursuit of excellence', they are 'to give of their best' and to focus 'on improving learners' achievement' (DfEE, 2001a, p2). All staff should share a similar vision and accept unreflexively given notions of excellence and continuous improvement. To do otherwise would be less than professional and to fail to own the institution's mission. To question or challenge these notions would reflect a failure to 'put the learner first'. In addition, there is the promise that those institutions that are on-message and successful will reap benefits and those that fail will be sanctioned (see DfEE, 2001).

Although providers have a degree of autonomy over self-assessment, *The Common Inspection Framework* for post-16 education forms its basis, setting the context within which self-assessment documentation is constructed (ALI, Ofsted, 2001). This process assumes a construction of learning and teaching, as well as a model of management. Through processes such as these the parameters of 'good' teaching practice are developed, disseminated and policed; so too are the institutional relations within which lecturers are located. This can be seen in the pivotal role given to management in the development of continuous improvement (see ALI, Ofsted, 2001 p13; FENTO, 1999, 2000).

Leaders and managers are to 'set a clear direction' and are to measure the effectiveness of institutional practices. They are to set demanding targets to which they and their teachers will be held accountable, as well as ensuring that performance management, staff appraisal and reviews are effective in improving the quality of provision. Management are to ensure that the 'best value' principle is applied in securing resources and services and that these are efficiently and effectively used (ALI, Ofsted, 2001, p13). The TPI (DfEE, 2001) operates within a similar framework and has a clear resonance with practices that have addressed teaching and threshold payments in schools (Barber, 2001; West, 2001; Smyth and Shacklock, 1998; Smyth *et al*, 2000). The stated concern is to reward excellence, value expertise and to retain it in the classroom, thus leading to continuous improvement and raising the standards, particularly of those who have been marginalised.

The TPI is based on criteria payments in terms of the acquisition of qualification (criterion 1), engagement in continuous professional development (criterion 2), and finally, professional effectiveness (criterion 3) in relation to student participation, retention, achievement and progression (AoC, DfEE, 2001, p8). A variety of evidential sources can be drawn upon to assess whether the individual has met the particular criteria; these range from classroom observation, learner evaluation and satisfaction surveys through to statistical data on learner retention, participation and achievement. In relation to criterion 3, professional effectiveness requires:

> Demonstrating effectiveness by raising students' participation, retention and progress in accordance with FENTO standards and college strategic plans. [FENTO is responsible for defining teaching standards in the sector]

> Supporting others to raise standards in teaching and learning, particularly part-timers or staff new in post. (AoC, DfEE, p12)

The DfEE also suggests that colleges may seek to create an Advanced Practitioner grade and that such a person would meet the TPI criteria. The DfEE notes that:

> It would be important for colleges to ensure that Advanced Practitioners remain up to date in their subject, keep abreast of developments in teaching and learning, and continue to have a positive impact on the experiences of students. (AoC, DfEE, p17)

All of these practices resonate with the earlier work on the labour process which examined changing forms of professionalism within the Learning and Skills Sector. Much of this early work was set within the immediate post-incorporation era. Further Education colleges were incorporated in 1993 when funding was removed from local education authority control and placed under the aegis of the Further Education Funding Council, now superseded by the Learning and Skills Council.

Research into managerialism and the labour process in Further Education has largely examined this in relation to the immediate post-incorporation era. The move towards market and competitive relations in the early period has been seen as encouraging masculinist and bullying forms of management (see Kerfoot and Whitehead, 2000; Leonard, 2000). Much has been made of the impact of performance management upon conceptions of professionalism. Randle and Brady (1997a,b), amongst others, have dwelt upon processes of proletarianisation and the loss of professional control. It is suggested that lecturers currently experience far closer surveillance of their work and that spaces for autonomy have become severely circumscribed.

A performance culture, marked by an emphasis upon accountability, is hardly one in which risk taking or the development of creative problem solving will arise. Performativity, through its chain of targets, operates within a blame culture where accountability becomes a means by which the institution can discipline its members. Performativity is reminiscent of Fordist work relations in as much as the worker is under strict surveillance, attempting to render transparent the details of his/her practice. Performance management sits well with low trust, if not distrustful, work relations (Codd, 1999) and is at odds with current understandings of the knowledge economy, which emphasise fluidity, non-hierarchical team work and high trust relations. In spite of this, it is argued that performance management is a mechanism whereby institutional energy can be directed to priorities deriving from its mission and targets. In this way performance management operates to discipline and channel members into preferred directions and practices. The consequences of these management practices are well enough known in the English context: low morale and problems with the recruitment and retention of teachers. There have been a number of steps taken by the state to address these issues, key amongst which is the on going reform of teacher professionalism.

Reform of teacher professionalism

[This pamphlet] focuses on those at the heart of raising standards: the talented and dedicated professionals who staff our schools and teach our children. And *it signals a new era of trust in our professionals on the part of government.* [my emphasis] (Morris, 2001, p1)

This section addresses a number of related issues: the changing forms of management within the learning and skills sector, the re-thinking of teaching relations, and the state emphasis upon the skills and contribution of teachers to national competitiveness.

Managerialism – New Relations?

Recent work has suggested that bullying and masculinist forms of management within Further Education colleges have been to some extent tempered. Deem, Ozga and Prichard (2000) attribute this to the emerging feminisation of management as well as to the departure of the first wave of post-incorporation management (see also Cole, 2000, Hughes, 2000). Gleeson and Shain (1999), from a different position, point to emerging co-operative and collaborative relations developing within the sector, holding the excesses of marketisation in check. Drawing upon Seddon (1997), they suggest that at least some senior managers are striving towards a form of professionalism that opens up progressive possibilities marked by more collaborative relations. Such directions are reflected in the move away from institutional competition towards collaboration and partnership (see for example, DfEE, 1998). Within this context performance management can be portrayed as a more appropriate and nuanced mechanism to direct institutional practice, when set against market competition. Such practices serve to distance those involved, either as managers or rank and file, from the arbitrariness of management diktat. In this instance performativity becomes embodied in a régime of truth that refuses other conceptualisations of good practice.

These developments accompany new approaches to trust in educational management relations. There is some renewed recognition of teacher expertise in relation to pedagogy as well as to subject/disciplinary knowledge (see Morris, 2001). In addition there is a construction of the teacher as working with and directing the labour of others, such as learning assistants. 'Successful' teachers will be given some autonomy. It is in this sense that trust has been re-figured as these practitioners will be given a certain amount of freedom to direct their own practice and exercise a degree of creativity and innovation. However, this is conditional, being set within a performative structure which calls the practitioner to account. Success will enable a degree of autonomy, whereas failure will call forth closer surveillance (see Morris, 2001). It is important to recognise that the conditional trust that practitioners achieve is set within a context in which management has secured the right to manage. Thus, as part of the FENTO *Occupational Standards for Management in Further Education*, managers are to 'anticipate areas of resistance' which 'require knowledge of techniques for overcoming resistance' (FENTO, 2000, FA2.3).

Teaching relations

Emphasis is placed upon the individual learner, with the teacher's role being to facilitate learning. The teacher is to become an expert facilitator of learning and therefore should be able to access and use a range of learning resources and techniques, from classroom practice to the use of information communication technologies (ICT). Thus teachers will have

> the skills to plan and organise learning and the effective use of resources and learning technology (DfEE, 2001b, p3)

They will be able to

> Offer a range of flexible opportunities for learning including learning facilitated through information learning technology (FENTO, 1999, B3)

The result will be that

> our pupils are achieving higher standards than ever before, supported by a wide range of teachers and other adults, and by world class ICT giving them direct access to world-class teachers. (Morris, 2001, p 14)

Embedded within this is not only a model of the preferred teacher, but also a view of what constitutes good practice, both of which readily fold back into a technicist construction of teaching. Performance management enables the state and its institutional arm within management to direct practice. Paradoxically, these technicist tendencies can be seen in the emphasis placed upon research (see Avis,

2001, 2002; Bloomer and James, 2001). Teachers are to draw on research findings to shape practice. However, the best practice model of research presupposes that research can generate such models. For example, literature reviews that examine existing research, drawing out pedagogic models of 'what works' to be generalised throughout the education system, expose major difficulties. In the case of performativity and the re-definition of teacher professionalism, the preferred teacher is expected to be aware of such research findings and to enact them within their own practice; to do otherwise would be construed as less than professional. Those who oppose such a re-definition of teacher professionalism are seen as cynics or as examples of the 'forces of conservatism' – the self-serving professional (Avis, 2000). They are to be given no credibility and to have no place in a modernised education profession (Morris, 2001).

Re-thinking Trust

The move from simple modernity to reflexive modernisation calls for the deepening of democratic relations and the expansion of trust. This will enable teachers to examine critically their own and institutional practices. For Leadbeater (1999) dissenting cultures underpin creative institutional responses to conditions of radical uncertainty; but for this to be expressed requires institutional relations of trust that authorise such dissent. In circumstances where uncertainty is all pervasive, top down authoritative relations are construed as counter productive and contrary to the conditions in which people work effectively. New Labour's interest in trusting teachers can be seen as a rather thin and chimeric version of trust.

Leadbeater suggests that trust is 'a lubricant for knowledge creation: people share and act on ideas when they trust one another. Trust and co-operation are as critical to success in a modern economy as self interest' (1999, p150). He further argues that low trust relations lead to high-cost management and administrative procedures. A similar position has been adopted by Kay (1996), which can be compared with those arguments that have called for the development of co-operative relations between companies in, for example, research and development. The Rhineland model of capitalism embodies these types of relations (Albert, 1994). However the success of this model of capitalist development is uneven and subject to the play of market forces. Leadbeater notes that in many analyses the notion of trust has been over simplified; this can be seen in the ready association of high trust relations with competitive success. He argues that high trust relations do not necessarily lead to competitive advantage, and that it is mistaken to associate trust solely with long-term relations.

What has this to do with re-thinking the nature of trust in education? On one level Morris' recent intervention, as well as those concerned with the softening of managerial relations, can be seen as an attempt to modernise the teaching profession to align it with contemporary conditions. In this case the concern with professional accountability can be thought of as similar to the portfolio worker who is given autonomy and trusted to deliver a particular task, and then moves to the next project where the ground rules need to be re-established. Although this description seems to embody Fordist, if not neo-Fordist work relations, another way to examine these would be to contrast them with those of legitimated teacher professionalism (Grace, 1987). This was in place for much of the post war period, until undermined by Thatcherism and the New Right in the 1970s. This model of pro-fessionalism de-politicised the classroom but also utilised a model of teacher autonomy that viewed teachers as curricular experts who knew what was best for their pupils. As a result of the ideological work of the New Right in the 1960s and 1970s, teachers were seen as having illegitimately introduced politics to the classroom; along with other state professionals, they were accused of being self-serving. The trust that underpinned legitimated teacher professionalism was lost.

Conclusion – the re-formation of teacher professionalism

The current moves in relation to teacher professionalism can seen as an attempt to re-moralise and re-construct teaching and to address the crisis that surrounds the profession. It is here that the notion of trust plays a significant part. Teachers are to be trusted to use pedagogic expertise and disciplinary knowledge to enhance standards and facilitate learner development, supported by ICT and learning assis-tants. They will be trusted to exercise some autonomy, innovation and creativity, all of which will be informed by knowledge of pedagogic practice and awareness of the findings of evidence-based research, which will provide models of best practice. The trust won at this level will have been achieved through performance management and be subject to on going review. I am reminded of the arguments of Beck (1999) and Bourdieu (1998), who suggest that risk has been passed further down the social structure so that the costs are carried by those at the bottom of organisational hierarchies.

Teachers' new professional relations are set within a context of conditional trust. This is very different to that of legitimated teacher professionalism in which the notion of collegiality sat alongside models of the teacher researcher: models deriving from the immediacy of practice and not constrained by a technicised understanding of best practice (see Carr and Kemmis, 1986; Avis, 2001). The latest form of professionalism operates within a model of trust that sees the teacher as a trusted servant rather than an empowered professional. Trust is located within a scenario in which performance management establishes the context in which the teacher is to act; evidence based research shapes pedagogic practice. This notion of trust is impoverished, in that it attempts to make the teacher conform to the diktat of the state. It is also an attempt to overcome teacher antagonism and opposition to crasser forms of managerialism. This is not a plea to return to an earlier model of professionalism, which itself was flawed. The goal should not be to re-instate this but rather to move towards a dialogic construction of professionalism, marked by democratic relations not undermined by spurious notions of performance management, or by similarly doubtful neo-market relations.

The condition of reflexive modernisation provides the base from which to develop a progressive professionalism. This can be glimpsed in Ranson and Stewart's (1998) discussion of the learning democracy, in which the resolution of manufactured uncertainty arises through the development of a democratic politics based upon civic engagement. Similarly, Brown and Lauder (2001) consider current economic conditions to be both enabling and requiring the development of an expansive professionalism. Such developments would derive from the struggle to widen democratic relations. The recognition that professional relations based upon performativity are seriously flawed has led to a demand for the development of a professionalism based upon a deliberative politics, marked by dialogue and negotiation across a range of constituents with an interest in educational processes (Codd, 1999). The work of Nixon *et al* moves towards a dialogic politics that recognises difference and incommensurable interests, and views deliberation as a way of resolving conflict (Nixon, 2001; Nixon, *et al*, 2001; Nixon and Ranson, 1997). There is a tendency in these approaches to veer towards a consensual if not pluralistic model of the social formation, one in which differing interests and incommensurable, difference can be harmonised through dialogue (Mouffe, 1998). Whilst recognising difference and incommensurability these authors are tied to Habermassian conceptions of rationality, which associate dialogue with an ideal speech community. In such a community power has no place, as it distorts the democratic relations that enable reasoned dialogue. These issues can be resolved in a professionalism that seeks to engage in dialogue but that recognises antagonisms present in wider society, and attempts to resolve difficulties by drawing upon an ethical commitment to social justice that recognises that not all differences can be harmonised through dialogue. If we take reflexive modernisation seriously and the radical uncertainty that surrounds it, a democratic and dialogic form of professionalism will be appropriate to address the educational problems of our time.

Acknowledgement

This is an edited and shortened version of a paper that appeared in the *Journal of Education Policy* vol 18 no 3, 2003, p315-332, http://www.tandf. co.uk/tf/02680939.html

References

Albert, M (1994) *Capitalism against Capitalism*. London: Whirr

ALI (2001) *Draft guidance on Inspection for providers: interpreting the common inspection framework*. Coventry: ALI

ALI, Ofsted. (2001) *The Common Inspection framework for inspecting Post-16 education and training*. Coventry: ALI

Avis, J (1993) A New Orthodoxy, Old problems: post 16 Reforms, in: *British Journal of Sociology of Education* Vol. 14, No 3, 1993 245-260

Avis, J (2000) The forces of Conservatism: New Labour, the third way, reflexive modernisation and social justice, in: *Education and Social Justice*, Vol 2, No 3, p 31-38,

Avis, J (2001) Educational Research, the Teacher Researcher and Social Justice, in: *Education and social Justice* Vol 3 No 3, p34-42

Avis, J (2002) Really useful knowledge? Evidence-informed practice, research for the real world, in: *Post-16 Educator*, Issue 8 March-April, p22-24

Avis, J, Bloomer, M, Esland, G, Gleeson, D, Hodkinson, P. (1996) *Knowledge and Nationhood; Education, politics and work*. London: Cassell

Barber, M (2001) High expectations and standards for all, no matter what: creating a world class education service in England, in: Fielding, M (ed) *Taking*

Education Really Seriously: dour years hard labour. London: Routledge Falmer

Beck, U (1992) *Risk Society: towards a new modernity.* London: Sage

Beck, U (1999) *World Risk Society.* Oxford: Polity

Blair, T (2001) Speech by the Prime Minister – the Rt Hon Tony Blair MP – at the CBI's National Conference in Birmingham, 5 November. http://www.cbi.org. uk/ndbs/press.../

Bloomer, M, James, D (2001) Research for educational practice: the promise of the transforming learning cultures in further education project; paper presented at the fifth annual conference of the learning and skills research network, Robinson college, Cambridge, 5-7 December

Bourdieu, P (1998) *Acts of Resistance: Against the new Myths of our time,* Oxford: Polity

Brown, P (2001) Globalization and the political economy of high skills, in: Brown, P, Green, A, Lauder, H (eds) (2001) *High Skills: Globalization, competitiveness and skill formation.* Oxford: Oxford University Press

Brown, P, Green, A, Lauder, H (eds) (2001) *High Skills: Globalization, competitiveness and skill formation.* Oxford: Oxford University Press

Brown, P, Lauder, H (2001) *Capitalism and Social Progress.* London: Palgrave

Callinicos, A (1999) Social Theory put to the test of politics, in: Pierre Bourdieu and Anthony Giddens *New Left Review* No 236 p77-102

Callinicos, A (2001) *Against the third way.* Oxford: Polity

Carr, W, and Kemmis, S (1986) *Becoming Critical.* Lewes: Falmer.

Codd, J (1999) Educational Reform, Accountability and the Culture of Distrust, in: *New Zealand Journal of Educational Studies,* Vol 34, No 1, P45-53

Cole, P (2000) Men, Women and changing managements of further education, in: *Journal of Further and Higher Education,* Vol 24, No 2, p203-215

Crouch, C, Finegold, D, Sako, M (1999) *Are skills the answer?: the political economy of skill creation in advanced industrial countries.* New York: Oxford University Press

Deem, R, Ozga, J, Prichard, C (2000) Managing further education: is it still men's work too?, in: *Journal of Further and Higher Education,* Vol 24, No 2, p231-250

DfEE (1996) *Competitiveness: creating the enterprise centre of Europe.* London: HMSO

DfEE (1998) *Further Education for the new millennium: response to the Kennedy Report.* London: HMSO

DfEE (2001a) *Raising Standards in Post-16 Learning: Self-Assessment and Development Plans.* www.dfee.gov.uk/post 16

DfEE (2001b) *Raising Standards: teaching in Further Education.* Nottingham: DfEE

DfES (2001) *Education and Skills: delivering results A strategy to 2006.* London: DfES

Giddens, A (1998) Risk Society, the context of British politics: Franklin, J (ed) *The Politics of Risk Society.* Oxford: Polity

Gleeson, D, Husband, C (eds) (2001) *The Performing School: managing, teaching and learning in a performance culture*. London: Routledge Falmer

Gleeson, D, Shain, F (1999) Managing the corporate education state: teachers and senior managers in FE as a case in point; unpublished mimeo

Grace, G (1987) Teachers and the state in Britain: A changing relation, in: Lawn, M, Grace, G (Ees) *Teachers: the culture and politics of work*. London: Falmer

Hall, G (2001) Keynote Address, presented at the fifth annual conference of the learning and skills research network, Robinson college, Cambridge, 5-7 December

Hughes, C (2000) Is it possible to be a feminist manager in the 'real world' of further education?, in: *Journal of Further and Higher Education*, Vol 24, No 2, P251-260

Husband, C (2001) Managing 'performance' in the performing school: the impact of performance management on schools under regulation, in: Gleeson, D, Husband, C (eds) (2001) *The Performing School: managing, teaching and learning in a performance culture*. London: Routledge Falmer

Hutton, W (1995) *The State we're in*. London: Jonathan Cape

Keep, E (1997) 'There's no such thing as society': some problems with an individual approach to creating a Learning Society, in: *Journal of Education Policy* Vol 12 N0 6 p457-471

Keep, E (1999) UK's VET policy and the 'Third Way': following a high skills trajectory or running up a dead end street?, in: *Journal of Education and Work*, Vol 12 No 3 p323-46

Kerfoot, D, Whitehead, S (2000) Keeping all the balls in the air: further education and the masculine/managerial subject, in: *Journal of Further and Higher Education*, Vol 24, No 2, p183-201

Lauder, H (2001) Innovation, skill diffusion, and social exclusion, in: Brown, P, Green, A, Lauder, H (eds) (2001) *High Skills: Globalization, competitiveness and skill formation*. Oxford: Oxford University Press

Lawn, M (1988) Skill in schoolwork: Ozga, J (ed) *Schoolwork: Approaches to the labour process of teaching*. Milton Keynes: Open University Press

Lawn, M (1996) *Modern Times: work, professionalism and citizenship in teaching*. London: Falmer

Leadbeater, C (1999) *Living on thin air*. Harmondsworth: Viking

Learning and Skills Council (2001) *Strategic Framework to 2004 Corporate Plan*, www.lsc.gov.uk/corporateplan.cfm

Leonard, P (2000) Gendering change? Management, Masculinity and the dynamics of incorporation, in: *Journal of Further and Higher Education*, Vol 24, No 2, p71-84

Morris, E (2001) Professionalism and trust – the future of teachers and teaching. A speech by the secretary of state for education to the social market foundation, 12 November, London: SMF

Mouffe, C (1998) The Radical Centre: a politics without adversary, in: *Soundings* Issue 9 Summer p11-23

Nash, I (2001) 'Deadly serious' cuts to red tape: *TES*, 23 Nov, p29.

Nixon, J (2001) 'Not without dust and heat': the moral bases of the 'new' academic professionalism, in: *British Journal of Educational Studies*, Vol 49, No 2, p173-186

Nixon, J, Marks, A, Rowland, S, Walker, M (2001) Towards a New Academic Professionalism: a manifesto of hope, in: *British Journal of Sociology of Education*, Vol 22, No 2, p227-244

Nixon, J, Ranson, S (1997) Theorising 'agreement': the moral bases of the emergent professionalism within the 'new' management of education, in: *Discourse: Studies in the cultural politics of education*, Vol 18, No 2, p197-214

Randle, K, Brady, N (1997a) Managerialism and Professionalism in the 'Cinderella Service', in: *Journal of Vocational Education and Training* Vol. 49 No 1 p121-140

Randle, K, Brady, N (1997b) Further Education and the New Managerialism, in: *Journal of Further and Higher Education*, Vol 21, No 2, p229-238

Ranson, S, Stewart, J (1998) The Learning Democracy, in: Ranson, S (ed) *Inside the Learning Society*. London: Cassell

Reich, R (1991) *The work of the nations: a blue print for the future*. London: Simon and Schuster.

Seddon, T (1997) Education: Deprofessionalised? Or reregulated, reorganised and reauthorised, in: *Australian Journal of Education* Vol 41 No 3 p228-246

Shain, F, Gleeson, D (1999) Under new management: Changing conceptions of teacher professionalism and policy in the further education sector, in: *Journal of Educational Policy*, Vol 14, No4, p445-462

Smith, A (1994) *New Right Discourse on Race and Sexuality*. Cambridge: Cambridge University Press.

Smyth, J, Dow, A, Hattam, R, Reid, A, Shacklock, R (2000) *Teachers' work in a globalizing economy*. London: Falmer.

Smyth, J, Shacklock. R (1998) *Re-making Teaching, ideology, policy and practice*. London: Routledge.

West, M (2001) Reforming teachers' pay: crossing the threshold, in: Fielding, M (ed) *Taking Education Really Seriously: dour years hard labour*. London: Routledge Falmer

Young, M (1998) Post-Compulsory education for a learning society: Ranson, S (ed) *Inside the Learning Society*. London: Cassell.

6

'Nobody told me there were schools quite like this': issues of power, discourse and resistance in writing about a school for emotionally and behaviourally disturbed (EBD) children

PAT SIKES AND JON CLARK

Two issues engage our attention in this chapter. Pat Sikes and Jon Clark give an account of education at an extreme: the extreme of physical danger and emotional stress in an environment where crisis management is the norm. It is an account intended to challenge the reader to reconsider fundamental issues: what is the purpose of education? What are educators expected to achieve, and why, and how? This chapter returns to issues raised in the earlier chapters – the general issues of government control raised in Part 1, and the more specific case studies in Part 2 (particularly Clegg and Ashworth) about the purposes of education and the monitoring of educational achievement. At the same time, the writers confront what they see as a 'major dilemma' of 'othering': 'that is, of re-presenting the school and particularly its pupils, as different and distinct'. They conclude that autoethnography may resolve the tensions inherent in this project.

NB. This paper is a collaborative endeavour and our use of 'we' and 'us' reflects this. Where 'I' is used we indicate which of us it refers to.

A Visit

I'd never been in a sports car before. Low and green and shining, pulling up for me in front of the tube station on a cold, wet Friday morning in December. It was the anniversary of my father's death and here I was, feeling excitement as I snucked into the seat. What a contrast with that morning in the hospital, eleven years ago, holding Dad's hand and waiting.

Jon accelerated down the high street, past the sari shops, the Asian grocers fronted with vegetable stalls, the Divali lights on the lamp posts. He drove fast, changing gear quickly, well over the speed limit. We turned into a council estate with speed bumps to fly over, traffic calming islands to weave round. He drives like this partly, I think, to get maximum exhilaration, partly to get back to school as soon as possible. He doesn't want to be away, doesn't want to miss the action or fail to deal with something that's his responsibility. He wants to get me there, to hear what I think. 'The police are coming in sometime this morning to get the security video of the incident I told you about when Zohab and his mates made the death threats to me and I'll probably need to have a word with them, but apart from that I'm doing nothing particular. What I thought was you'll just be around, talk with Harry, meet the kids, hang out. That OK?' 'Fine. I just want to see and to get some sense of what it's like for you.'

I'm enjoying the ride, the closeness to the road, the sense of being in touch. 'That's our field'. To my right I see a green space: the size of three football pitches or so. We turn in a gate, pink blossom out on the trees lining the drive, 'I arranged that because you were coming. Welcome to Osbourne.'

I sense he feels proprietorial and proud. I see a two storey, seventies building. Flat roofs, big windows, coloured panels. Obviously a school. The grounds are neat, close cut grass, tidy borders. And those blossom trees. In December.

We go in through the lobby to the reception hatch where I have to sign in. Banter with the secretaries who call him Jonty. He tells them I'm his teacher. They say I must have my hands full.

The corridor is bright, clean and carpeted. There's no graffiti on the walls, no scuffmarks on the skirting board, no litter on the floor. And it is very, very quiet. I comment on the quietness and Jon tells me it's not normally like this but today nearly half of the students are out on work experience and college placements, while some of the 'big players' incurred short term exclusions the previous day.

'Let me take you to meet the kids'. We turn into a corridor with classrooms off to either side, work displayed on the walls. A man comes out of a room.

'This is Pat'. I'm introduced to Harry, the principal. He's big, like Jon, but taller. They joke, slagging each other off, showing me their relationship. Harry tells Jon that while he was out the police rang to say that they'd just arrested Zohab, then says, 'You aren't going to like this but Peter's coming in later to check you're ok about the threats. The LEA's worried about you. They want to look after us so we have to let them'. He turns to me, 'See you later. I'll be interested to know what you think'

Jon takes a bunch of keys out of his pocket and starts to open the door. I'm surprised. 'Why is it locked? What if there's a fire?' 'The doors lock on the corridor side but you can get out from inside the room. If that wasn't the case, the one kid absconding from a class could force their way into other rooms and set the whole school off in seconds.'

It's suddenly noisy. 'You fucking cunt! Bastard! Your mother's a whore, she's a whore. Fuck you!' 'Don't you say that about my mother. *Your* mother's a cunt. Fuck *her*!' There are two big boys, about 15 years old, sitting either side of a hessian covered room divider. They're shouting at each other and banging about but they're still paying some attention to the workbooks on the tables in front of them. Each boy is accompanied by a middle-aged adult, who in both cases is telling them to attend to their work and stop shouting. In the middle of all this Jon simply introduces me as Dr Sikes, his teacher. I hold out my hand to every individual in the room and both boys stop their invective to take it and say hello. One asks me if it's true that I'm Jon's teacher, the other if he's a good student. I say yes. Then they go back to their cursing. Jon has some words to the effect that winding each other up is not a good idea then we go out and cross the corridor to a classroom where three boys of 13 or so are sitting round a table with two young women. They're all cutting out snowflake shapes from white paper. Gratuitously I ask if they're making Christmas decorations and a fresh-faced child holds up a mile of paper chains they'd made the previous day. His pride and delight remind me of my son when he used to show me things he'd made with his nanny whilst I was at work. It's calm, relaxed and purposeful in that room. Easy, as it can be when kids are doing work they enjoy, in the company of teachers they like and trust.

It's not quite so comfortable in the next room. There, four lads are playing a word game with two adults. Except one of the boys, Darren, has headphones on, is listening to music and is emphatically distancing himself from everything and everyone else. Jon asks him to take the headphones off. The boy deliberately turns his back on him. Jon puts his hand on the boy's shoulder and has a quiet word. 'It's time for pizza' says one of the other kids and everyone gets up. As he slouches towards the door, Darren removes his 'phones.

Then, suddenly, the bangs start. The walls of the corridor are being thumped, hard, so that they shake. There seem to be loads of youths out there, lots of shouting, fucking this and fucking that. I swear but I have never heard cussing like this. 'They get pizza now if they've been ok. Come along and have some.' A kid bumps into Jon 'Watch where you're fucking going Jonty', 'Language, Sam', 'Sorry'.

The dining hall is in another building. Outside the door stand Jon and Harry. Each boy has to pass by them and something is said to everyone. There's lots of hugging too. I've never seen so much physical contact in a school, not even in a nursery. It's odd, remarkable, to see these males, lads and teachers, touching each other so much and so naturally. In a mainstream school I'm sure it would provoke homophobic accusation and abuse.

After pizza Jon takes me to see the workshops and music room. On our way, the Learning Mentor has a word about a lad who is sounding off and getting upset because he wants to go in the music room and he thinks that the member of staff who has to accompany him there isn't going to. Suddenly the boy himself appears. He's clearly very wound up and angry. He strides round the hall area we're in, bashing the walls and the doors, swearing and bad-mouthing the teacher he believes has let him down. Three or four kids come to their classroom doors, peer through the glass then go back to whatever they were doing. I'm not sure what to do, where to go. This is outside my experience and I'm apprehensive. Jon talks to the boy, tells him the teacher will be along shortly, that the music session will happen if he calms down. The boy walks round and round the area, faster and faster, banging away all the time. Jon asks him to be reasonable, to remember positive things and suddenly it's all over as the lad says, 'I need a drink', goes over to the drinking fountain and drinks deeply. He returns, apparently ok now, then, quick as a wink shins up above the door and sits in the heating pipes, waiting for his teacher. Jon tells me later that this is a major advance, that a couple of months ago the anger would have continued to increase until he finally blew totally out of control. Going to the drinking fountain was a back down without losing too much face.

We enter the woodwork room. I'm very conscious of the hammers, chisels, and saws. A boy is standing at a bench, rhythmically stabbing away with a bradawl. Each time it goes further in until the handle hits the wood and he can't get it out. 'Fuck it. Stupid fucking thing.' 'What if somebody loses their temper in here?' I quietly ask the teacher, a man who's recently moved here from a mainstream school, 'Isn't it risky to have these tools out?' He shrugs, 'It's risky anywhere'. There's a knock at the door. Jon's needed to deal with a flare up in a PE lesson. I hear the shouting, the kicking and banging. This one takes a long time to defuse and by the time some understanding is reached it's lunchtime. Back to the dining hall and the hugs and the words to each boy before they go in.

Ross, a large lad with complicated braces on his teeth, is teased for never smiling. He stands close to Jon; I think he's seeking contact. 'Look, there's a policeman going into school. What's he here for?' Police visits could be bad news for most of the boys and Ross I'm told, does drugs and deals drugs big time. 'He's not a policeman, he's come to see to the photocopier.' 'He's a policeman. Look at his boots.' The man is, of course, the copper who's come to pick up the security video. All the school know about the threats and that there's a warrant out for the kids who made them. Jon goes off to talk to him.

While he's away an obviously pregnant teacher comes and tells Harry that she's been pushed by David who is now in the dining room. David's brought out and confronted with what he's done. There's some bravado but he ends up saying sorry and verbally, at least, acknowledging that he was in the wrong.

'Come and eat, the food's really good here'. It is. Ravioli, salad, ice cream, fresh fruit. Jon told me they're careful about the food they serve because many of the kids live on junk at home. Everything is fresh and as far as possible they ensure that there are no additives or colourings because these can aggravate hyperactivity. As well as pizza and lunch, Harry and Jon come into school at 6.30 and cook breakfast for those who turn up. Without this there are some who'd have nothing to eat in the morning and the number of kids who don't attend until pizza time would increase.

I sit next to a tall boy who sprawls round his chair and over the table. The staff sit around the room, some together, others with kids. There's a general and wide-ranging conversation going on that everyone seems free to participate in. My neighbour shouts his contributions rather than speaks them. He appears to be getting excited and gets louder and louder. Suddenly there's a startling bang as a boy behind me knocks his table nearly right over. It teeters on two legs then crashes down, rocking back and forth a few times. All is momentarily silent and then: 'Hey Sally, hey Sally! Sally's got fuck me shoes on. Show us your shoes Sal'. Sally who is about 25 and attractive and who teaches drama here and in Wandsworth prison, laughs and gives back banter. It all seems well meant and harmless, a comment on the style of her footwear rather than anything else. Jon and Harry appear to think so too: at least they say nothing to stop it and indeed, themselves join in.

'Time to get back.' Harry signals the end of lunch and kids and staff slope off to lessons. The afternoon session is short: school ends at 2.30. Some don't even make it that far and, in any case, if they've done well they're often allowed to go early. Given the past attendance record of many of the boys, it's an achievement to have them come in at all.

It's time for me to hear the story of the school. We go to Harry's room, a large office, dominated by a picture of Cassius Clay before he was Mohammed Ali, triumphant having beaten Sonny Liston. Harry opens a drawer in his desk and invites me to look inside. There are a number of knives, razor blades fixed to various makeshift handles, a length of bicycle chain, a sharpened screw driver, and a couple of chisels. 'These were all confiscated during my first weeks here. I keep them to remind me not to get too cocky. Keep them in mind while I'm talking'. The story goes like this: in January 2001, Osbourne, a residential school for 11 to 16 year old boys with severe emotional and behavioural difficulties, was put into Special Measures following an Ofsted Inspection. What the Inspectors reported made such lurid reading that journalists on the tabloids seized the opportunity for sensationalist headlines of the '*Is this the worst school in England?*' variety. The Ofsted report was immediately removed from the DfES web site as it began to register an unprecedented number of hits. Those who managed to get there before it was withdrawn learnt of incidents of boys gang-raping other boys on the school premises, of a hanging, of numerous woundings with weapons, of staff who were demoralised or complacent or incapable, of drug taking, of a school population where the majority of pupils had criminal records, and of an all-pervasive macho, violent culture.

Faced with this damning report the LEA had decided to close down the school, sack most of the staff, and then re-open it minus the residential unit, under a new name, and with a new régime. Harry was appointed to lead this renaissance with Jon as his deputy. After one term they felt that they were beginning to get somewhere.

Their shared vision is to create a caring environment with a culture that provides certainty, constancy and security for boys who, for various reasons, do not behave in a way that can be accommodated in mainstream schools. Many of the boys have learning difficulties; some have mental, emotional and psychological disorders, others have attention deficit conditions. Most of them come from disadvantaged backgrounds, some have been involved in child prostitution, a few have parents with learning difficulties and a large number have grown up with criminal activity – thieving, prostitution, violence, drug taking – as the norm. All are a potential threat to themselves and usually to other people. Their futures are not promising and, at the time of the Ofsted report, 80% of those on roll were involved with the youth justice system with a further 12% serving or awaiting custodial sentences.

These kids are a complex amalgam of power and vulnerability. In their immediate lives they have power, which they use to hurt and damage people and property. Within the wider world they are relatively powerless and most even lack the personal characteristics needed to be a successful criminal. As children too, they are incredibly vulnerable, and a number of them are known to be exploited and abused sexually, physically and emotionally by their parents and/or other adults who should be caring for and protecting them. In some cases this vulnerability is heightened by the adoption, perhaps as a survival strategy, of a hard man persona that is manifested through their demeanour, their clothes, the music they make it known they listen to, and their language. Many parents who teach see their own children in the students they encounter. For staff at Osbourne who are also parents, this experience is particularly poignant.

Jon talks of 'cutting off the balls and drawing the teeth' of the culture that had come to characterise Osbourne before he and Harry arrived. Their mission is to show their students an alternative way of being to that which they have either been socialised into or have come to adopt and which was being reinforced pre-Ofsted. In doing this they are engaging with and living through issues of power, discourse and resistance. For themselves, and for their students, this involves the acknowledgement of personal and social power and vulnerability. It means providing unconditional love and a clear framework of ways of behaving based on respect for people and property. For many of the boys this is a novelty and they are having an experience they haven't had before, either at home or in schools they have attended. Hence the touching – an obvious demonstration that 'I care about you'; hence the demand that kids reflect on and acknowledge the impact of their actions on other people and themselves; hence the importance given to respect for self and others; hence the emphasis on corporate responsibility and the well being of all people belonging to the school.

They think that it's beginning to work. Kids have said things that indicate that they enjoy coming to school and attendance levels are up. When a teacher's purse was stolen Ross showed Jon the dog shit bin where it had been dumped, because 'I like the school'. Louis cried and apologised for bashing Jon against a door and badly winding him; and after Zohab threatened Jon (threats the police took seriously knowing the crowd he hung round with) a number of the kids came up afterwards to ask if Jon was OK.

But it isn't all success of course: Wayne, who stole the purse, and Zohab, who said he would kill Jon and get his family are both pupils. Truancy remains a problem. And, desperate and dreadful though the action is for boys who have nowhere else to go to but prison, two permanent exclusions have been made. Nevertheless Harry and Jon do seem to have begun to make a difference – and an interim report by LEA inspectors suggests that coming out of Special Measures now seems a certainty.

'What's your impression of Osbourne?' 'Nobody told me there were schools quite like this. If I hadn't been here I couldn't have imagined it'. 'I know what you mean' says Jon. 'When I was at college and even when I was doing my Masters I never came across anything in the academic literature that even began to describe what it can be like here. The most you get is something along the lines of 'working in these institutions is demanding and requires resilience'. It's all distanced and sanitised and pretending to be objective. There should be stories that give you a sense of the feel of such places, stories that tell you what they're like for the people in them. That's what I'm trying to do. Why don't you write about it too?'

A mid-point sort of introduction

There was no *Introduction* to this chapter because we wanted to try and share, without the dilution of any preamble, something of what it felt like to visit an EBD school for the first time. We also hoped that readers would see for themselves various issues relating to discourse, power and resistance embedded in the substance and form of the narrative rather than being directed to see them by an *Introduction*. Of course, there are contradictions in, acknowledging on the one hand, as we do, that all texts are capable of multiple readings, while on the other, saying 'we hope that you make this particular interpretation' (see Bochner and Ellis, 1996, p15). Authorial strategy, let alone power, cannot guarantee any reading! Having said this, it is now widely accepted that social scientists do influence interpretation by the language and structures they use and therefore have an ethical and moral responsibility to choose their words carefully. In the remainder of this chapter we will be reflecting on the ethical dilemma of othering that we experienced around re-presenting perceptions and experiences of life at Osbourne, and also touching on considerations of what constitutes legitimate academic research and writing: questions around what Denzin and Lincoln refer to as the 'triple crisis of representation, legitimation and praxis (*that*) confronts qualitative researchers in the human disciplines (2000, p17).

Re-presenting Osbourne

For us, a major dilemma in bringing Osbourne into the public domain is one of othering (see Fine, 1994): that is, of re-presenting the school and particularly its pupils, as different and distinct from other schools and pupils. Making exotic, appropriating through description and thereby dehumanising the people on whom their gaze turns has ever been an issue for those who study and write about aspects of human life and society. But the extent to which this has been recognised as an issue and as an ethical problem has varied, depending upon the positioning of the researcher and upon historically, culturally and socially located understandings (see Geertz, 1973, 1983).

The dilemma is not made any easier because there are differences, albeit socially constructed ones, between EBD schools and their pupils and mainstream schools and theirs. Our aim is not to highlight or emphasise these differences *qua* differences. Conversely, in telling a story about a sector of education that many people know little about, our intention is, in the broadest sense, inclusionary. In other words, knowing something about schools like Osbourne and the kids who attend them can give insights into 'how much *out there* looks like *in here*' (Neumann, 1996, p182) and allows them to be included in our knowledge, understanding and awareness of the world. This is the reverse of 'othering'.

'Othering' happens partly as a result of the language used to depict the people and settings we are describing. As Wittgenstein noted, the choice of particular grammars and vocabularies reflects the choice of particular realities (1968). The choices that we make concerning the nature, form and types of re-presentation we adopt have implications for the people we are writing about (see Fine *et al*, 2000), the audiences we reach, the type of understandings we communicate, and also for how our work is located in terms of academic respectability and legitimacy (Richardson, 1997). These implications fundamentally concern power: power, for good or ill, to impact upon the situation and the people we are researching and writing about, and power within the academy.

When the tabloid press picked up on Ofsted's report on Osbourne and translated its official language into lurid journalese, considerable interest was provoked. If we as researchers/academics are of the view that it is impossible to unequivocally re-present reality, that 'writing is not an innocent practice (*and*) in the social sciences there is only interpretation' (Denzin, 2000, p 898), we have to acknowledge that we are in exactly the same relationship as are journalists with regard to our words and the effect these have on our readers. This puts us under an ethical obligation to explain why we wrote the first part of the paper as a story that included verbatim reports of pupils' obscene language and described disturbing behaviour. Without such a justification we could well be accused of exploiting vulnerable and disturbed children in order to attract attention and titillate an audience. It is worth noting here that the day Pat visited Osbourne was considered by all staff to have been 'quiet', with nothing exceptional occurring: there was no 'great story' (Fine *et al*, 2000, p117) to report.

Imaginative contact and autoethnography

So why have we used this narrative form? Primarily because we believe that writing that aims to convey some sense of what it can feel like to be at an EBD school stands a better chance of making 'imaginative contact' with readers (see Goodson and Sikes, 2001, p50) than does the traditional academic style. Associated with this view are our beliefs and values relating to our role as academics, researchers and writers (see Sikes and Goodson, 2003). Perhaps, though, we should start by explaining why we come to be writing about Osbourne at all and why, in doing so, we have used a style that follows Laurel Richardson's call to 'writing-stories (that) are both personal and political... (That) situate (our) work in socio-political, familial and academic climates' (2001, p34). To do this we need to go back to 2000 when Jon started a four year taught doctorate (EdD) programme. During the last two years of the course, students undertake a research project, usually related to their professional concerns, that is reported in a 50,000 word thesis. Getting the job at Osbourne halfway through the course meant that Jon's original research plans were no longer viable. In addition, knowing the amount of time and commitment the work was likely to demand he questioned whether it was going to be possible to continue with the degree. At this point he came to talk to Pat, the programme Director. After some discussion, it seemed that an autoethnographic investigation was the answer.

Coffey describes autoethnography as 'ethnographic writing which locates the self as central (*and in so doing*) gives analytical purchase to the autobiographical' (1999, p 126). Autoethnographers put themselves into their text whilst locating these texts in the literatures and traditions of the social sciences (see Ellis and Bochner, 2000; Lather and Smithies, 1997; Richardson, 2000). Autoethnography had potential to help Jon reflect critically and systematically on his work, leading him to insights and understandings capable of informing his professional activities and also serving as a cathartic outlet for the tensions and stresses he was likely to face. An autoethnographic account of being vice-principal of Osbourne could make an original contribution to understandings concerning special and inclusive education, re-starting failing schools, and qualitative methodologies. Consequently Jon produced a research proposal entitled *Restarting the 'Worst' School in the Country: An Autoethnographic Account*. Data for the project would take the form of reflective and reflexive accounts written over the academic year 2002–2003. Pat received the first instalment, *Every Day Feels Like Friday. Every Friday Feels Like The End Of Term*, in mid-November.

I had never read anything concerning a teacher or a school like it before. Jon had written vividly and persuasively (Baronne, 1995), re-flexively and analytically about his initial expectations, impressions, and experiences of Harry, the school, pupils and staff; about his hopes, intentions and anxieties for himself in the job; about the vulnerability and the 'badness' of the kids and their behaviour at school, at home and in the community; about his family's coping with his pre-occupation; about the physical demands that restraining pupils made on his body and the injuries he had sustained; about the exhaustion and complexity of doing the job. His writing made me feel that I had to see this school and meet these kids for myself, both to broaden my knowledge and awareness and to enable me to better understand the nature of Jon's research endeavour. It had, in a very real way, led me to an inclusive experience and perspective. In writing this chapter as we have, our intention is to create a sense of place and people, pro-voke imaginative contact and enable readers to have a similar type of experience. That people who have worked in EBD schools have said our account 'takes them back' suggests some degree of success.

Amanda Coffey writes about the necessity of recognising that 'fieldwork is personal, emotional and identity *work*' (1999, p1). Jon and I are fully cognisant of the auto/biographical grounding and nature of our perceptions, experiences and re-presentations of Osbourne and believe this awareness enables critical subjectivity. This is particularly the case for Jon who sees his research as praxis that 'seeks emancipatory knowledge [that] increases awareness of the contradictions hidden or distorted by everyday understandings' (Lather, 1986, p260) Through autoethnography, Jon hopes to empower himself by becoming a more effective practitioner. He also hopes to be awarded a doctorate and yet, even these days, submitting an autoethnography as a doctoral dissertation is not without risk. In deciding to take this approach, in doing research of this kind and in writing in a explicitly storied fashion, Jon and I feel we are engaging with questions of discourse, power and resistance in a very immediate and personal fashion. Earlier we quoted Denzin and Lincoln's reference to the 'triple crisis of representation, legitimation and praxis [that] confronts qualitative researchers in the human disciplines' (2000, p17). This chapter is our start at addressing that crisis.

References

Baronne, T (1995) Persuasive Writings, Vigilant Readings and Reconstructed Characters: The Paradox of Trust in Educational Story Telling, in: Hatch, J and Wisniewski, R (eds) *Life History and Narrative*. London: Falmer, pp63–74

Bochner, A and Ellis, C (1996) Introduction: Talking Over Ethnography, in: Ellis, C and Bochner, A (eds) *Composing Ethnography: Alternative Forms of Qualitative Writing*. Walnut Creek: AltaMira, pp13–45

Coffey, A (1999) *The Ethnographic Self*. London: Sage

Denzin, N (2000) The Practices and Politics of Interpretation, in: Denzin, N and Lincoln, Y (eds) *The Handbook of Qualitative Research: Second Edition*. Thousand Oaks: Sage, pp897–922

Ellis, C and Bochner, A (2000) Autoethnography, Personal Narrative, Reflexivity: Researcher as Subject, in: Denzin, N and Lincoln, Y (eds) *The Handbook of Qualitative Research: Second Edition*. Thousand Oaks: Sage, pp733 – 768

Denzin, N. and Lincoln, Y. (2000) Introduction: The Discipline and Practice of Qualitative Research, in: Denzin, N and Lincoln, Y (eds) *The Handbook of Qualitative Research: Second Edition*. Thousand Oaks: Sage, pp1–28

Fine, M (1994) Working the Hyphens: Reinventing Self and Other in Qualitative Research, in: Denzin, L and Lincoln, Y (eds) *The Handbook of Qualitative Research*. Thousand Oaks: Sage, pp70–82

Fine, M, Weiss, L, Weseen, S and Wong, L (2000) For Whom? Qualitative Research, Representations and Social Responsibilities, in: Denzin, N and Lincoln, Y (eds) *The Handbook of Qualitative Research: Second Edition*. Thousand Oaks: Sage, pp107- 131

Geertz, C (1973) *The Interpretation of Cultures: Selected Essays*. New York: Basic Books

Geertz, C (1983) *Local Knowledge: Further Essays in Interpretative Anthropology*. New York: Basic Books

Goodson, I and Sikes, P (2001) *Life History in Educational Settings: Learning From Lives*. Buckingham: Open University Press

Lather, P (1986) Research as Praxis, in *Harvard Educational Review*, 56(3): 257–277

Neumann, M (1996) Collecting Ourselves at the End of the Century: Ethnography, in: Ellis, C and Bochner, A (eds) *Composing Ethnography: Alternative Forms of Qualitative Writing*. Walnut Creek: AltaMira, pp172–198

Richardson, L (1997) *Fields of Play: Constructing an Academic Life*. New Brunswick: Rutgers University Press

Richardson, L (2000) Writing: A Method of Inquiry, in: Denzin, N and Lincoln, Y (eds) *The Handbook of Qualitative Research: Second Edition*. Thousand Oaks: Sage, pp923–948

Richardson, L (2001) Getting Personal: Writing Stories, in *Qualitative Studies in Education*, 14(1): 33–38

Sikes, P and Goodson, I (2003) Living Research: Thoughts on Educational Research as Moral Practice, in: Sikes, P, Nixon, J and Carr, W (eds) (2003) *The Moral Foundations of Educational Research: Knowledge, Inquiry and Values*. Buckingham: Open University Press

Wittgenstein, L (Tr Anscombe, G) (1968) *Philosophical Investigations* (Third edn). New York: MacMillan (first published 1953)

7

Constraining bodies: inspection as a form of hygiene

VALERIE REARDON

In this chapter, Valerie Reardon makes a creative and provocative link between the regimentation and sanitisation of the female body and the processes surrounding the punitive inspection régime within the UK education system. Echoing the concerns of Stronach, Lather and Newby in Part 1, over government intervention in education, and Avis's critique in Part 2 of notions of professionalism, performativity and trust, Reardon draws on the discourses of feminism and psychoanalysis and on the work of Mary Douglas to explore notions of purity and danger in the context of the educational panopticon.

Introduction

The central idea for this chapter is that an analogy can be drawn between the current culture of accountability in education – particularly as it manifests in régimes of inspection – and the policing of the female body in which largely implicit cultural rules and representations govern what constitutes a clean and proper femininity. This somewhat attenuated coupling came to mind during my experience at a large Further Education college in the UK where I was lecturing on a postgraduate teaching programme that certified teachers for the post-compulsory (16+) sector. In the UK, the legal school leaving age is 16 and entry into university or Higher Education does not usually occur until the age of eighteen. Further education colleges were traditionally focused on vocational provision for students sixteen and over, but they are increasingly seen as bridging the gap between school and university and many now incorporate Higher Education (degree level) courses. Further Education provision (as distinct from Higher Education) is, however, subject to the same process of inspection as schools. As many of our PGCE (Postgraduate Certificate of Education) students were teaching on FE courses at the College, I witnessed firsthand the effects on them of the institutional preparations for an impending Ofsted inspection. (The acronym Ofsted stands for the Orwellian title: Office for Standards in Education). With increasing dismay I saw their stress levels rise and their spirits fall, but it was the intensification of management proscriptions, coupled with a proliferation of increasingly bizarre signage in the women's lavatories, that gave me the idea for this chapter.

It occurred to me that the disciplinary régimes manifest both in the Ofsted inspection and the lavatory signs coalesced around the notion of hygiene. We know very well what the feminine ideal produced by cultural discourse looks (and smells) like, but how can a focus on hygiene help us to understand the whole machinery of inspection, standardisation and homogenisation of which Ofsted is but a tiny part? By drawing on feminist and psychoanalytic understandings of sexuality and subjectivity, as well as on the work of the anthropologist Mary Douglas, I am able to argue that what I consider to be the pathology of inspection, particularly as it is articulated through the dichotomy visible/invisible, has its roots in the fear of and fascination with sexual difference.

According to psychoanalytic theory, the recognition of sexual difference is fundamental to the formation of subjectivity. This is because the taking up of subjectivity requires the subject to speak as an 'I' and, as Lacan (1979) argues, the 'I' is always gendered. Although the truth value of psychoanalysis has been frequently critiqued, many feminists have utilised psychoanalysis in order to assert that gender is psychically constructed, not biologically given. Furthermore, it is worth pointing out that the seeming play on words between 'I' and 'eye' is not merely accidental, as the two terms, one abstract and the other anatomical, are dynamically interwoven in the founding of sexed subjectivity. The phallus, as the symbolic form of the anatomical penis, is the master signifier of sexual difference, in that it is the sight of who has or does not have the phallus that sets the criteria for the sexed distinction between masculine and feminine. Within this differentiation, the sight of the female genitals is no sight at all, as there is nothing to see. As Luce Irigaray argues (1985:48):

> Nothing to be seen is equivalent to having no thing. No being and no truth. The contract, the collusion between one sex/organ and the victory won by visual dominance therefore leaves woman with her sexual void, with an actual castration carried out in actual fact.

Freud considered both boy and girl to be bisexual until they experience the vicissitudes of the oedipus and castration complex. His account of the acquisition of masculine and feminine subject positions traces a trajectory through the oedipus complex in which the (male) child gives up his love for the mother when he realises that she does not possess the phallus and, consequently, fears that he could lose his as well. For Freud, the oedipus complex structures male sexuality by privileging the penis/phallus – that which can be seen – as the only viable sex organ. The deduction that females lack this influential appendage not only structures female sexuality as absence or lack but it also makes them represent for the male the threat of his own castration. Clearly, there is a lot at stake in the visible. If what cannot be seen poses such a threat we can begin to understand why there is such an emphasis on presence, power and surveillance in current inspection processes.

Inspection as both a concept and a process concerns the monitoring and surveillance of the visible. Like Foucault's model of the panopticon in *Discipline and Punish* (1991), the mechanism of continual surveillance habituates us to internalise the practices and values of inspection, whether or not we are being watched. Not only do we become self-policing, but embedded in the inspection process is our assumed cooperation in policing our peers and colleagues. Teachers must be seen to teach and students seen to learn but for the most part, during the period of official inspection, both groups collude in what is commonly understood as a performance. Grounds are planted, buildings are cleaned up and painted, pictures and framed mission statements are hung in the corridors. It's like a royal visit but without the Queen, whose benign and smiling countenance bestows on her subjects a sense of their unified place in history. For participants in Ofsted (particularly the majority of the teaching staff) no such luxury is on offer.

The most successful institutions in Ofsted terms (and success is rated on a point system) are the ones best able to present a sanitised and hygienic vision of the often disorderly, unpredictable and chaotic business of education. The notion of purity that is embedded in the word hygiene depends for its meaning on the suppressed but equally evocative notion of contamination. Derrida (1978) reminds us that language is constructed from the violence of binary opposition in which the dominant term – in this case hygiene – is always predicated on an opposite, but subordinate term. Meaning, however, is never quite so clear cut, but is the product of an endless chain of signification. The subordinate term, suppressed within the dominant meaning, is not only unspoken but also often unthought, and therefore subject to unconscious processes of repression and displacement.

If we bring this understanding of the underside of language to the meaning and practices of hygiene, we can begin to see its fetishisation as a symptom of unconscious fear. Of course, it can be argued that very real notions of hygiene underpin medical science. One would not, for instance, want to be operated on by a barehanded surgeon who had just amputated a gangrenous limb. But the signs in restaurant bathrooms that insist, 'Now wash your hands' depend for our compliance on an inchoate fear of invisible, and thus presumed dangerous, bacteria. This imperative speaks volumes, not least about the assumption of a shared cultural code that defines cleanliness as next to godliness.

To establish an identity predicated on purity, whether as an institution or a woman, resonates with the sacred in ways that I would suggest are incompatible with the contemporary educational environment, at least in post-compulsory education and training in the UK. And yet the instrumentalist practices associated with régimes of inspection embody an almost biblical privileging of the visible. The exhortation 'Let there be light' sets up the demand for clarity and vision that underpins Christian culture, while simultaneously relegating to the darkness (and the unseen) all manner of evil. The process of inspection makes a similar demand in that teaching and learning must at all times be visible. Furthermore, evidence of that transaction has to be codified in lesson plans complete with ostensibly verifiable learning outcomes. Such a clearly technical-rational economy however discounts the immeasurable internal processes of learning, the learning that can't be seen, let alone immediately articulated. In his discussion of teacher-student interchanges, David Scott (2001:4) proposes that one way of thinking about the purpose of that exchange is to

> dissolve, fragment and otherwise disrupt the models of knowledge held by the student, and, at best, the teacher. Here, there is no attempt made to provide a replacement, since the purpose is to provide disjuncture in the minds of the students, and the responsibility for replacement is devolved to the student.

The kind of teaching Scott describes resonates with my own experience, yet I would find it difficult to reify that process in ways that would be meaningful to Ofsted. To initiate the student-teacher exchange with a set of 'learning outcomes' that can be verified at the end of the class nullifies the kind of multi-faceted, peripheral learning that education is, in my view, meant to be about. It also forecloses the possibility that good teaching might just mean that the teacher is equally open to the possibility of learning in the classroom.

During the months leading up to an inspection, classes are observed, often by strangers, and pre-defined checklists largely govern the feedback given. The use of a variety of teaching aids and strategies such as white boards, group discussion, flip charts, and overhead projectors is seen as evidence of good practice. Presentation techniques can easily take precedence over content, in response, presumably, to those dubious questionnaires that allegedly determine 'learning styles' – often the educational equivalent to astrology. Schemes of work and lesson plans that break down teaching and learning activities into five-minute intervals are required of all teaching staff. A young lecturer whom I interviewed told me he had been working an average of eighty-six hours a week producing retrospective paperwork. 'I wouldn't mind if the time was spent preparing for teaching' he said, 'but as it's not, the process has left me de-motivated, disillusioned and demoralised'. The fetishisation of paperwork that has become integral to the 'quality assurance' process has become so normalised within the audit culture that few bother to question either its veracity or its purpose. As Fred Inglis (2000:422) reminds us, it is the production of codified proof that dominates everything else:

> The bureaucratic rationality that animates the practical articulation of accountability holds that duties are subordinate to rights, and the determination of rights-fulfillment is only secured by tabulation. A

right is satisfied when evidence is produced not so much that the duty has been done, but that the documentation on hand codifies its doing.

Rob, the lecturer I interviewed, told me that when the inspection was first talked about he 'looked forward to it', assuming that it would provide an opportunity for frank and collegial discussion about such things as the curriculum and the resourcing of his department. He soon realised his naivety when it became clear that he was being told what to say about what he 'produced' and how he produced it. This coincides with my own experience of receiving an e-mail outlining what must and must not be said to the inspectors who were currently on the premises. A notion of hearty team spirit is evoked (don't let the side down) but in fact, such an e-mail interpellates the recipient as a potential threat, rather than a valued member of a team. Rob described himself and his colleagues as previously 'working effectively together despite limited resources' but the pressure of complying with the increasing demand for evidence meant that they no longer had the time to speak to one another. He felt that he had no voice in the inspection process because to raise the issue of inadequate resources, for instance, was constructed as tantamount to treachery.

Another effect of this demand for visible evidence is to undermine the teachers' confidence about taking the kinds of creative risks that engender spontaneity and enable them to respond more flexibly to the rough and tumble, here and now of classroom practice. The increasing demand for documentation, largely produced under pressure and with resentment, constructs us all as somehow failing in our duties. It is as if for all those unknown exemplary others, the production of this kind of visible evidence is woven into the fabric of their teaching practice. To disregard it, because it is at best stultifying and at worst unreliable, is to be not only faulty, but also suspect. This presumption of failure is compounded not only by the fact that observation feedback is often graded, but also because the practice itself suggests a lack of trust about what it is that occurs when we are left to our own devices in the privacy of the unobserved classroom. If surveillance practices such as these are left unchecked, the resulting homogenisation of teaching will not only leech all vestiges of creativity from the profession; it will also deprive students of the rich panoply of teaching styles and personalities that enrich (and sometimes enervate) the learning process. Accountability in this form is all about mastery of the visible, driven by the fear and imagination of all that cannot be seen.

Fear of what cannot be seen was nowhere more apparent than in the signs that began appearing in the women's toilets as the date for the Ofsted inspection drew closer. These notices initially exhorted the occupants to 'please flush the toilets and not leave litter around'. But escalation in the form of sanctions began when a lavatory used primarily by female students was locked for two days running. I investigated this closure after receiving complaints from the students, only to be told that they were locked because they had been left in a 'disgusting state'. Further enquiries produced the information that an empty crisp packet had been found on the floor. Clearly, the drive for hygiene was becoming pathological. The following week, new signs appeared in the female staff toilets, which read as follows:

> Could you please
> ensure that
> sanitary towels
> are put into the
> bins provided and
> not left lying
> around the toilets
> Thank you for
> your cooperation

Signs asking women to dispose of their sanitary protection in the bins provided are fairly commonplace and usually motivated by a concern for the plumbing. In this case, however, it was the extension into the graphic image of bloody towels scattered on the floor that caught my imagination, particularly in the context of what was really a pristine lavatory. Who was the anonymous author? And what kind of vivid and fearful imaginings was he or she subjected to? Sitting in the cubicle, the sign served to structure me as a guilty female. Or if not me, then who among my colleagues was given to such filthy practices?

In her seminal work of 1966, *Purity and Danger*, the anthropologist Mary Douglas outlined the many ways in which cultural taboos, predicated on the fear of impurity or 'filth', are manifested in different societies. Douglas makes the point that the weaker or more threatened the centre of any social organisation perceives itself to be, the more formalised the rituals and taboos are likely to become. In other words, there is a distinct correlation between social control and fear. But do the Ofsted inspectors grade us on the state of our lavatories? If not, then what are the signs about?

The dichotomy founded on anatomical difference, culturally articulated as masculinity and femininity, is the source that structures all other binary oppositions. Mind/body; culture/nature; active/passive; rational/irrational: each pair is assigned by lateral association to the sexually explicit categories of masculine/feminine. Binary oppositions are always ordered hierarchically: thus culture is the dominant term to nature, active to passive, rational to irrational and of course, male to female. The correlation and association of Woman (upper case and in the singular) with the body, and Man with the mind is, according to Elizabeth Grosz (1994:4) 'not contingent or accidental but central to the way in which philosophy has historically developed and still sees itself even today'. A concept of the body as irrational and essentially disordered underpins the disembodied rationality that drives the inspection-as-hygiene process. Furthermore, while the masculinised mind is associated with transcendence, the feminised fleshy body is inscribed with death through the processes of aging, illness and disease. As Elisabeth Bronfen (1992:67) writes

> Woman's body is seen as polluted, as fatal to the masculine touch, an agent and carrier of death. Because Woman is used as an allegory for that deterioration of flesh which the surviving subject wishes to deny, yet knows is his destiny, the beauty of Woman is conceived as a mask for decay...

So the signs in the lavatories are symptomatic of an economy of fear that has death at its root and the female body as its sign. What Bronfen is arguing is that the correlation between Woman and the body is necessary in order for Man to maintain the illusion of immortality. He expels knowledge of his own death by making the female body, by virtue of its association with reproduction (and thus, nature) stand as the sign of death and decay. Understood in this way, it is easy to see how the preoccupation with feminine beauty and hygiene is consistent with a cultural denial of death. Beauty serves as the mask that hides death's secrets, and we only have to consider our fascination with the tragic deaths of beautiful young women, from Ophelia to Princess Diana, to understand how the beautiful young female corpse serves to arrest and deny the processes of ageing, decrepitude and inevitable mortality. Because the vulnerable body carries within it the potential disorder of death, it must be disciplined and controlled if the illusion of immortality is to remain intact. In the same way, the disciplinary practices of school, 'school' both students and teachers in order to maintain illusions about democracy, equality and the 'natural' order of things, suppressing the obverse inequities of late Capitalism.

While female beauty masks death and decay, it is the female body as essentially polluted that is of more immediate relevance to the subject of hygiene. The shame and secrecy surrounding menstruation have no origin in any real threat of disease and yet, as Mary Douglas outlines, rituals and taboos concerning menstruation are predicated on the notion that menstrual blood is a dangerous pollutant that must be excluded in order for a social group to see itself as clean and proper. Menstrual blood as a form of filth or defilement is an element connected with the boundaries and margins of the body. As Elizabeth Grosz (1994:203) points out:

> the female body has been constructed not only as a lack or absence but with more complexity, as a leaking, uncontrollable, seeping liquid; as formless flow; as viscosity, entrapping, secreting; as lacking not so much or simply the phallus but self-containment.

The association of femininity with death and disorder, the uncontrollability of the limits of the female body, its fatal attraction and strong revulsion, are all common themes in cultural representations. Social rituals act primarily to counter wavering certainty by protecting society from the cognitive discomfort caused by ambiguity. Ambiguous things can seem very threatening in that they destabilise the drive for order and certainty that structures rationality. Epistemological systems presume that in order to know the world, it is necessary to classify its phenomenological parts by defining typological boundaries between one thing and another. The more complex taxonomies one can cite, the more knowledgeable one is considered to be and yet, as with the binary oppositions that structure language, there is always a repressed and thus threatening state of indeterminacy that undermines the anxious certainty of the grid.

Douglas's anthropological study reveals the role of ritual and taboo in shoring up a symbolic system that is under threat. Douglas discovered that a social symbolic system, as articulated through ritual and taboo, corresponds to a specific structuration of the speaking subject in the symbolic order. In other words, as speaking subjects, we are constrained to the degree by which the dominant group in the social system we inhabit perceives itself to be threatened. In societies that are structured around notions of the sacred, these constraints take the form of ritual and taboo. In the secular culture of British education they take the form of inspection, audit and accountability.

In his brutally insightful indictment of the current culture of accountability, Fred Inglis (2000:424) describes it as replacing 'the inevitably messy give-and-take of human dealing':

> Accountability is, after all, not the same thing as responsibility, still less a duty. It is a pistol loaded with blame to be fired at the heads of those who cannot answer charges. (*Ibid*)

The almost hysterical emphasis on hygiene and bureaucratic control that surrounds the Ofsted process suggests a fear of pollution, contamination and chaos that is more the product of paranoid imagination than anything grounded in reality. The binary oppositions that structure meaning are always hierarchical and the dominant term defines itself by expelling its other, and, in this process, establishes its own boundaries and borders to create an identity for itself. Thus, a crucial aspect of identity is founded on the expulsion of all that is somehow unacceptable or even unknowable to itself. Understood in this context, the disciplining technologies and practices that make up the identity of Ofsted raise important questions around the nature of the terrible things that are only vaguely imagined about just what it is that we do when we are teaching unobserved. Passion and emotion, historically aligned with the (female) body, have no place in the branded New Labour British identity that sees itself as technically-rationally modern and in control. The technical rational imperative is predicated on an economy of cause and effect that fails to take into account the 'messy give and take of human interaction'. The privileging of the visible, as evidenced by the régime of bureaucratic and punitive surveillance embodied in Ofsted, presupposes that there is a mortal danger in that which cannot be seen. It is easy to argue that this kind of totalitarian certainty has a chilling parallel with the recent war on Iraq, motivated, as it allegedly was, by the supposed existence of weapons of mass destruction that had been allegedly 'hidden'.

Despite the constraints imposed on us by the audit culture described in this chapter, there are grounds for optimism. As educators, we must take heart from the knowledge that although we are marginalised in a market-driven culture that sees teaching as a fairly peripheral but begrudgingly still necessary service within the central dyad of client-consortium, we nonetheless occupy a position of strength, due to the very fact of our marginalisation. As marginalised others, far from the controlling certainty of the centre, we inhabit a space of indeterminacy and ambiguity, rich with potential for boundary transgressions. Seeping and leaking beneath the grid, we can move from one category to another, potentially transforming all we come into contact with. Neither liquid nor solid, we can be hard to pin down, blurry, out of range and often out of sight. And by challenging the festishisation of hygiene that mistakes tidy desks (and lavatories) for effective teaching, we might bring to the Ofsted inspectors' attention Mary Douglas' prescient observation that dirt is only matter out of place.

References

Bronfen, E (1992) *Over her Dead Body: Death, Femininity and the Aesthetic.* Manchester: Manchester University Press

Derrida, J (Tr Bass, A) (1978) *Writing and Difference.* London: Routledge and Kegan Paul

Douglas, M (1966) *Purity and Danger.* London and New York: Routledge

Foucault, M (Tr Sheridan, A) (1991) *Discipline and Punish: The Birth of the Prison.* London: Peregrine Books, Penguin

Grosz, E (1994) *Volatile Bodies: Toward a Corporeal Feminism.* Bloomington and Indianapolis: Indiana University Press

Inglis, F (2000) A Malediction upon Management, in *Journal of Education Policy,* 15(4): 417-429

Irigaray, L (Tr Gill, G) (1985) *Speculum of the Other Woman.* Ithaca, New York: Cornell University Press

Lacan, J (Tr Alain- Miller, J) (1979) *Four Fundamental Concepts of Psychoanalysis.* London: Penguin Books

Scott, D (2001) Situated Views of Learning, in: Paechter, C, Edwards, R and Harrison, R (eds) *Learning, Space and Identity.* Buckingham: Open University Press

PART THREE
NEW MOVES: WIDENING PARTICIPATION

8

From Freire to fear: the rise of therapeutic pedagogy in post-16 education

KATHRYN ECCLESTONE

Kathryn Ecclestone returns in this chapter to the issue of the 'therapeutic ethos' raised by Dennis Hayes in the first volume of this series. She argues that an unhealthy preoccupation with health – specifically, the emotional wellbeing of the student – gets in the way of learning, with stultifying consequences for the learner and teacher alike, creating 'a new sensibility that resonates with broader cultural pessimism about people's fragility and vulnerability'. Ecclestone is far from recommending 'an uncaring view of some people's lack of confidence or vulnerability'. Her challenge is to the facile notion, which she sees as sharply at odds with the resilience so powerfully advocated by Freire, that esteem should be conferred upon a passive learner by an education system more or less exclusively preoccupied with issues of identity and emotional wellbeing.

Introduction

In a recent discussion about a meeting where a colleague had been forceful in his opposition to a proposal, another colleague explained his anger as the product of low self-esteem, adding 'he's actually a very fragile person'. In a conversation with a colleague about a grievance being brought by a female secretary against a male professor who was behaving aggressively and unreasonably, the colleague representing the secretary used the university's code on bullying to argue that she had suffered depression in the past, for which she had received counselling and that she has low self-esteem. Far from addressing the professor's unacceptable behaviour, this tactic diminished the woman and merely appealed to his sympathy, or worse, his pity. There is also a discernible increase in the numbers of my university students citing their low self-esteem as a barrier to being challenged or receiving feedback. Amongst friends, colleagues and students generally, the language of stress, traumatic or offensive experiences, distress and feeling abused or violated is much more commonplace than even two or three years ago.

These personal examples of concern about people's vulnerability are reflected in popular culture and the media. For example, a search of 300 UK newspapers in 1980 had no references at all to 'self-esteem', three in 1986, 103 in 1990 and 3,328 in 2000 (Furedi, 2003: 3). Celebrity chat shows and confessional television, such as *Parkinson* and *Oprah Winfrey*, revel in therapeutic analyses of people's traumas, the permanent scars of childhood experiences, and identity crises. Celebrities such as David Beckham are praised for being open about their vulnerability, while public sector workers increasingly present themselves as 'being ordinary' and uncertain, rather than heroic or brave (Campbell, 2003; Sarler, 2003). In America and Britain, there has been an exponential rise in the numbers of psychotherapists, counsellors and guidance workers across the public sector and in private practice. It seems that the language, symbols and codes of therapy now permeate all areas of cultural and political life in America and Britain (see Nolan, 1999; Furedi, 2003 for detailed analysis).

Concerns about self-esteem are prevalent in Britain's education and welfare systems. For example, the Socialist Education Alliance argues that real progress for education can only be made by longer term investment in the foundations of the education system: in building the self-esteem of all our children (Cole, quoted by Hayes, 2003: 35). In a similar vein, the Assessment Reform Group emphasises stress and damage to self-esteem as one of the most pernicious effects of national testing, rather than the use of tests to rank and differentiate people for social and educational opportunities (2002). The National Institute of Adult and Continuing Education regards low self-esteem as one of the most important barriers to participation and achievement for adults and therefore an area for educational diagnosis and intervention

(James, 2003). Building self-esteem is an official goal in education programmes for young mothers and their children, drug education in youth work settings, initiatives to raise the self-esteem of 'non-traditional' entrants to higher education and in personal mentoring systems for disaffected, 'hard to reach' young people and adults (Surestart, 2002; DfES, 2002a, 2000b; SEU, 1998).

More broadly, the British government under New Labour has created widespread agreement in all areas of public policy that social exclusion is inextricably linked to destructive influences that damage self-esteem (Blair, 1997). In Labour's 'Third Way', the welfare state is crucial in supporting people's psychological well being and is regarded by policy makers as a source of esteem (see Giddens, 1998). Across diverse policy spheres, from education and welfare to neighbourhood renewal projects, museums and community arts projects, policy makers and professionals hope to build individual and communal self-esteem (see Furedi, 2003).

Yet, despite the apparent common sense and caring concern that underpins claims that self-esteem and educational attainment are connected or that low self-esteem causes a wide range of life problems, there is no conceptual clarity or conclusive evidence about these claims (see Emler, 2001; Furedi, 2003). In America, the Californian state government commissioned research into self-esteem, and found no conclusive evidence for the construct or its effects, let alone instruments that could measure it. The commission that produced the report acknowledged these problems but nevertheless made raising self-esteem amongst its population a key goal in state education and welfare services (Nolan, 1998; Furedi, 2003). According to Emler, the political and popular position in America and Britain comes close to that of confessional television host Oprah Winfrey, who argues that 'low self-esteem is the cause of all the problems in all the world' (Emler, 2001).

Lack of clarity and conclusive evidence about self-esteem mean that, according to Furedi, it has acquired the status of a cultural myth which now exerts a strong hold over popular, professional and political thinking at all levels of American and British society (Furedi 2003). If this is so, it raises the question of why there appears to be growing concern in educational debates about people's vulnerability and emotional well being. This chapter aims to address this question by exploring the rise of 'therapeutic pedagogy' in parts of the post-16 system. It examines the features and roots of therapeutic pedagogy and evaluates its implications for professional roles and educational aspirations.

1. The rise of therapeutic pedagogy
a. A therapeutic ethos

Elsewhere, I explored the nature and effects of a 'therapeutic ethos' in public and cultural life and its implications for post-16 education (Ecclestone, 2004). I summarise the main characteristics of a therapeutic ethos from that paper here before going on to explore its translation into pedagogy.

One feature of a therapeutic ethos is the now commonplace application of therapeutic interventions in more areas of public and personal life. From trade union activity on stress and bullying through health and safety at work policies, to the routine use of trauma counsellors after crises and proposals by the National Society for the Protection of Children for counsellors to be employed in all schools, direct applications of therapy are commonplace across British social and welfare policy, as well as in education and welfare interventions in international aid programmes (Furedi, 2003; Pupavac, 2000).

While an increase in direct therapeutic interventions is discernible, a more subtle therapeutic ethos is emerging from these interventions and in culture more generally. This offers particular symbols, codes and ways of thinking about what it means to be human and these permeate everyday discussions of behaviour and relationships, thereby changing our perceptions of what being human means and our beliefs about people's capacity for moral agency. A therapeutic ethos re-shapes the boundaries of moral life (see Nolan, 1998) and offers what Furedi calls a 'cultural script' for interpreting how we respond to life events and our own development. This privileges individualism and emotion as the main justifications for actions and behaviours, thereby replacing older notions of guilt and responsibility. Nevertheless, a therapeutic ethos admits some emotions as culturally acceptable (being open about vulnerability, for example) and others as unacceptable (such as showing anger (Furedi, 2003).

A more insidious effect is to replace older tenets of humanism, such as the potential for personal transformation, responsibility and trustworthiness (Rogers, 1961, 1986) with less hopeful ideas about human nature. According to Furedi, older forms of respect for resilience, resistance to adversity and aspirations for the future have been replaced by fears about the future and about risk, leading to cultural empathy for 'the diminished subject', namely the idea that people are victims of their circumstances, rather than authors of their own lives (Furedi, 1997). A pessimistic view of the world and of humanity's ability to solve problems underpins the diminished subject (see also Malik, 2000).

Negative images of dysfunctional people, together with ideas about lasting emotional or psychological damage caused by a growing range of everyday behaviours, has led to the pathologising of a very wide and growing range of emotional states, disorders, syndromes, addictions and dysfunctional categories. The American Psychological Society now lists over 800 that cause physical symptoms and explain a growing range of behaviours from the most commonplace and mundane to the most extreme or rare (Nolan, *op cit*). According to Furedi, similar trends are evident in the UK. His analysis of media, professional and political coverage of crime and health, the exponential rise of therapeutic processes and symbols across cultural life, together with moral panics about parenting and adulthood, lead him to argue that risk consciousness, anxiety and a preoccupation with people as helpless victims of circumstance. Personal histories all fuel a therapeutic culture and intensify the professionalisation of emotional and private life (Furedi, 1999; 2001; 2003).

Nevertheless, it is important to recognise how new social problems change people's sense of their own agency and that of others. In particular, old forms of communal support, trust and networks provided by communities, unions and workplaces have all but disappeared in many areas, creating serious psychological and social problems. Educators experience intensifying regulation, the decline of collective resistance, the casualisation of working conditions in post-16 sectors, and political expectations that they should be able to solve intractable social and personal problems. Like youth workers and social workers, they are on the front line of motivating and retaining more people who suffer from profound disadvantage. Stephen Ball argues that the pressures of performativity clash with teachers' beliefs and values, creating fear, anxiety and feelings of helplessness that are internalised and individualised (2003). Therapeutic responses seem to signal concern for people experiencing distressing life and work pressures, whilst suggesting that more aspects of life are stressful and problematic.

Nevertheless, although this chapter is critical of a therapeutic turn in responses to structural and political pressures, arguments developed below should not downplay these pressures or their psychological effects. Nor should arguments in this chapter suggest an uncaring view of some people's lack of confidence or vulnerability, or imply a wholesale rejection of therapy and counselling for particular problems. Instead, this chapter aims to explore the subtle, insidious effects of a therapeutic ethos that extends symbols of damage, fragility, dysfunction and vulnerability to an otherwise mentally well, resilient population. The impetus for this chapter is a deep concern that pessimism about our ability to function effectively, together with the suggestion that life itself makes us vulnerable and psychologically unwell, lead to diminished ideas about our own professionalism and students' capacity for agency.

b. Educators' interest in esteem and identity

An important question is whether empathy with a diminished self, promoted through a therapeutic ethos, creates new ideas about pedagogy. There does seem to be a more therapeutic sensibility in current ideas about identity and self. For example, Valerie Hey draws upon Ulrich Beck's widely cited analysis of the reflexive individual coping with a 'risk society' to argue for the importance of understanding identity formation in relation to gender and class. She regards 'psychological capital' as crucial to understanding these dimensions, arguing that this type of capital 'differentiates us' because it is formed by our unique memories, emotions, feelings, desires, rage, shame, resentment, power, pain and pleasure (Hey, 2003: 324). For Hey, exploring these concerns enables public discussion of the 'splits, shifts and dislocations' involved and is politically compelling because it recasts the 'stigma and shame of difference as voice' (*ibid*: 331). Educational transactions rooted in identity offer 'immediate (therapeutic) recognition' and, are an empowering response to the disappearance of public discourses of class and class action and their replacement by the compulsion for 'an intensely individualistic, self-regulating, responsive identity' (*ibid*: 329).

These ideas draw on feminist and radical traditions that encourage democratic processes for mutual learning,` where teachers are equal participants in 'confessional narratives' (hooks, quoted by Preece, 2001, p10). For educators committed to the transforming power of education, 'starting where learners are' is a spring-board for subverting or challenging prevailing norms and structures, challenging how people's identities have previously been constructed and confined by power structures and discourses, and creating new identities (see Jarvis, 2001; Burn and Finnigan, 2003). Some educators see the notion of self-esteem as a focus for promoting social justice. For example, Morwena Griffiths argues that the notion of self-esteem enables students and teachers to question how life experience meshes with material outcomes of inequality to produce collective forms of low self-esteem, thereby challenging the typical presentation of self-esteem as an individual pathology (see Griffiths, 2003).

Other post-16 educators seek to place students' concerns and their learning careers at the heart of an empowering curriculum and democratic, trusting partnerships between teachers and students (see, for example, Bloomer, 1997; Harkin *et al*, 2000). For Burn and Finnigan, individual experience, the emotional dimensions of identity, biography and students' own narratives challenge elitist forms of assessment, teaching, oral and written critique in Higher Education that damage learners' self-esteem and silence academics and teachers from non-traditional backgrounds. From this perspective, pedagogy resists the imposition of teachers' authority and academic conventions and subverts the division between the rational and emotional. In this scenario, *producing shared stories is a political act* (Burn and Finnigan, 2003: 132) and a starting point for critical understanding of the ways in which institutional practices and policies validate certain types of students at the expense of others (see also Hey, *op cit*).

In response to instrumental, regulated curricula, pedagogies of resistance emerge by helping teachers and students understand how *signs, images and virtual representations of everyday life construct us in particular ways* (Baudrillard, cited by Gale, 2003: 173). The joint creation of maps and journeys to explore these constructions resonates with interest in educators' professional identity as something that is always fragmented, fractured and in process (Harrison *et al*, 2003: 61). From this perspective, pedagogy helps individuals analyse how identity is discursively constructed through everyday metaphors, symbols and language. In a similar vein, opportunities to explore biography and identity enable professional educators to reach out authentically to communities which suffer from collective low self-esteem (see, for example, Gordon, 2003).

b. Radical roots

The ideas summarised above have clear roots in critical and radical traditions, and are presented as part of a commitment to social justice and empowerment. Yet, reference to the influential ideas of Catholic Marxist and liberation theologist, Paulo Freire, illuminates the intro-spective, emotional and pessimistic turn that seems to be emerging in these ideas. In Freire's vision of critical liberal education, 'safe spaces' enable teachers and learners to explore the 'lived experience' of indivi-duals and the group through mutual problem solving and co-learning, as spring-boards for empowering social groups to fight oppression (Freire, 1999; 1994). For Freire, learners and teachers need to relate these processes directly to the political, social and cultural conditions in which they operate. In his context, the repressive conditions of Brazilian society and politics during the 1960s and 1970s meant that pedagogy, and the social and personal goals that underpin it, had to be embedded in a specific context for change, such as rural agricul-tural projects for learning literacy.

The ideas of Freire are widely cited by adult educators across the world, although perhaps more often as symbols of an affinity with a radical tradition than as a deep reading of their political implications. His influential text, *Pedagogy of the Oppressed* is required reading in many post-16 teacher education courses in the UK, alongside Rogers' *Freedom to Learn*. Yet, his optimism about a 'vision for tomorrow', without which hope is impossible (1997), contrasts starkly with con-temporary concerns with pessimism and vulnerability. For example, Beck's influential thesis of a risk society reflects growing scepticism about expertise, pessimism about progress and the future, lack of trust in personal and social life, and the decline of civic engagement. Despite Beck's belief that risk is the motor of new forms of democracy and self-politicisation, his overall thesis and prognosis for a risk society are profoundly gloomy. For example:

> Whereas the utopia of equality contains a wealth of *substantial* and *positive* goals of social change, the utopia of the risk society remains peculiarly *negative* and *defensive*. Basically, one is no longer concerned with attaining something 'good' but with *preventing* the worst; *self-limitation* is the goal which emerges. The dream of class society is that everyone wants, and ought to have a *share* of the pie. The utopia of the risk society is that everyone should be *spared* from poisoning (Beck, 1992: 49, original emphasis).

2. A de-politicised pedagogy
a. Verbal radicalism

The low aspirations of the risk society resonate with those of therapeutic pedagogy, despite the emancipatory rhetoric in both sets of ideas. It is also possible to interpret a shift from critical pedagogy towards a therapeutic interpretation from the passion and personal openness of Freire's work, which suggests that personal narratives and identity formation are a legitimate, substantive curriculum around which teachers can construct dialogue and mutual problem solving. Yet, from Freire's intensely politicised understanding, personal narratives, personal reflection, openness about mistakes, dilemmas and doubts are merely ways to understand one's own journey as a person, political activist and educator within a broader context and to evaluate one's role in social transformation. Far from being introspective, critical pedagogy aims to embed such processes within teachers' and students' understanding of a specific cultural and political context, particularly in relation to the potential for political action (Freire, 1994).

In order to stress the importance of a sophisticated political understanding, Freire re-evaluated his earlier ideas in the 1990s to take account of the disintegration of the political left and the uncertainty and new oppressions created by global capitalism. He also updated insights into the Brazilian context in which his earlier ideas evolved. Although he argues that we cannot underestimate fears caused by tighter forms of neo-liberal globalisation, and the depoliticisation of the left, he argues that:

One of the differences between me and fatalistic intellectuals – sociologists, economists, philosophers or educationalists – lies in my never accepting, yesterday or today, that educational practice should be restricted to a ... 'reading of the text' but rather believing that it should also include 'a reading of context', a 'reading of the world', and in hope and a critical, in no-way-naïve optimism (1997: 43-44).

However, reiteration here of Freire's ideas about political context in critical pedagogy should not imply a naïve, nostalgic belief that old ideas can simply be resurrected for new times. Instead, the aim is to show that pessimism about risk, low expectations of progress and a diminished sense of self all erode hope for social transformation and politicisation. At the same time, postmodernists seem to portray such hopes as deluded arrogance arising from old 'grand narratives'. Such trends arise from, and contribute to, professional demoralisation (Ecclestone, 2004).

It is far from clear how, in response to pessimism and demoralisation, introspective pedagogy resists or subverts power, except within a narrow context of classroom relationships. While the nuances of personal identity and its construction are absorbing in some way as therapy is, it is not clear what material and social consequences these concerns have. This means that although supporters of therapeutic pedagogy espouse a strongly radical rhetoric, their ideas are divorced from any substantial political analysis of the potential, or otherwise, for social change. Hayes argues that in the UK those advocating a new therapeutic pedagogy exaggerate the potential for social and political change that lies within the hands of students, by failing to analyse social and political conditions created by the New Labour government. Instead, a rhetoric of democracy and emancipation masks a serious political retreat into *comfortable verbal radicalism* (2003: 38).

According to Furedi, the collapse of the left has led to a flight from belief in personal and social transformation and a fatalistic acceptance of vulnerability (2003). In a de-politicised context, notions of 'safe spaces', 'making learners visible on their own terms', 'creating new identities' and 'privileging the learners' voice' take on a distinctly introspective tone. They appear to provide a source of comfort and personal engagement in situations that are impersonal, oppressive or alienating. Yet, by echoing cultural interest in the 'diminished subject', therapeutic pedagogy offers well meaning reassurances of inclusion divorced from a political and ideological context and therefore without moral commitment (see Ecclestone, 2004).

b. Ghettoising low-risk education

Supporters of critical pedagogy regard education as a means through which people define and conduct their own struggle for recognition in a specific historical, political and cultural context. In contrast, calls by policy makers and state agencies to recognise and affirm the esteem and equal worth of everyone are made *on behalf of* marginalised groups. For Furedi, this removes aspirations that people construct history in their own struggle for recognition because, although such calls appear to have a moral tone, they are abstracted from social and cultural aspirations for recognition (2003). A vicious circle emerges, where low expectations for those deemed to suffer from low self-esteem produce more claims by educators on their behalf and embed psychological deficiency into educational beliefs about people. The more students are encouraged to engage with a therapeutic ethos, the more likely it is that the radical rhetoric of safe spaces merely creates comforting processes without substantive content. A more insidious implication is that once a therapeutic mind set takes hold amongst professionals, *a person's emotional state is ...no longer a personal matter but becomes public property and related to the responsibilities of citizenship* (Pupavac, 2001a, p361). Following this argument, well meaning calls to confer recognition eventually deny society and individuals their moral capacity.

These effects sideline structural explanations of problems and divert effort into exploring people's emotional responses to social and political problems, rather than to trying to solve them. New forms of dependency on external agencies for help with experiences and events once dealt with by family, friends and local communities undervalue resilience, positive risk and agency. These tendencies create *an excessive focus on state intervention... rather than sources of protective influences that lie within individuals, families and communities* (Newman and Blackburn, 2002: 7). Newman and Blackburn argue that in place of collective resilience, popularising self-esteem through education and welfare persuades a generation of young people that self-esteem is the route to success, thereby presenting social barriers to progress as psychological ones (*ibid*). A therapeutic pedagogy also creates a closer alignment between welfare, judicial and educational interventions (Nolan, 1998; Ecclestone, 2004).

Such dangers make it important to question *which* groups of people are characterised as having low self-esteem. For example, recent policy proposals for youth work target unemployed and working class youth as being at risk of suffering oppressive behaviour such as bullying and peer pressure, caused by low self-esteem (DfES, 2000b). Similarly, the Social Exclusion Unit characterises particular groups as victims of the cycle of deprivation and a wide range of emotional and social problems (SEU, 1998; Colley and Hodkinson, 2003). Educators therefore need to ask whether therapeutic pedagogy could become an educational ghetto of introspection for some adults and young people, while those not deemed to suffer from low self-esteem or to be at risk carry on developing useful cultural and social capital.

For some learners, then, education could become little more than a series of unchallenging experiences and interventions that probe their identity, diagnose their levels of self-esteem and explore emotional responses to life events. In addition, if identity is discursively constructed and if giving voice to people offers immediate recognition, it becomes extremely difficult to challenge espoused theories and low expectations of achievement or to offer constructive feedback in case these activities threaten esteem. These dangers can be summarised through two old liberal and critical slogans, namely 'start where learners are' and 'the personal is political'. Therapeutic pedagogy runs the risk of stopping at the personal, thereby leaving people in the same place as they started.

3. Diminishing professionals
a. New bonds with a disaffected public

A therapeutic ethos enables state agencies and professionals to reinvent themselves in ways more relevant to prevailing media, political and popular concerns (Nolan, *op cit*). Far from seeing claims for recognition and esteem as a threat to its authority, the state has embraced them because the psychological well being of subjects offers new bonds with a fragmented public (Furedi, 2003). Following this argument, a therapeutic ethos offers new ways to govern professions where *the passions, identities, collectively shared meanings and moral dispositions within the 'lifeworld' of the social actors (rather than their economic interests)... need to be changed'* (Offe, quoted by Dale, 1998: 280).

Yet a therapeutic ethos engages with the passions and identities of educators by emphasising their vulnerability. For example, Ball argues that demoralising, insidious performativity alters teachers' identity and professionalism in profoundly distressing, traumatic and emotional ways that are experienced and internalised individually (2000; 2003). The danger of a pessimistic, diminished response to the effects of regulation is reinforced by Beck's vision of a risk society which sees professionals as having to legitimise their activity through openness and self-criticism as the basis for democratic dialogue (Beck, 1992). In his chapter in the present volume, Avis suggests, following this argument, that since policy makers and the public no longer trust the professionalism of post-16 teachers, but hold them tightly accountable, openness must be a basis for new dialogues with interested constituencies if professionals acknowledge conflicting interests between them.

The problem is that invoking notions of terror, fear, anxiety and vulnerability brings therapeutic symbols into the heart of professionals' own accounts of themselves, thereby running the risk of using a diminished identity as the basis for creating shared meanings and dialogue with the public. Empathy with students, for example, based on disclosures of vulnerability, or a damaged identity, is a diminished basis for being open and self-critical in order to gain the trust of a disillusioned public. A diminished professionalism that prioritises the conferment of recognition and esteem is likely to have unanticipated negative effects. Not least, if professionals define themselves and the people they work with as suffering from low self-esteem and unable to deal with external and self-induced problems, a sense of individual and collective helplessness takes hold.

b. From Freire to fear

In this chapter, the notion of a therapeutic ethos seems to offer part of an explanation for educational concerns with self-esteem and identity. In particular, these trends suggest a new basis for therapeutic governance and legitimation in education in the UK (see Ecclestone, 2004). Yet professional fear or pessimism may also have other roots. In his analysis of the basis for respect between public sector workers and their clients, sociologist Richard Sennett argues that professionals have to deal with 'invidious comparison', namely resentment and de-motivation in the face of both unequal talent and unequal oppor-tunities (2003: 94). He argues that modern policies such as personal mentoring or impersonal forms of affirmative action seek to counter invidious comparison that wounds the self. For him, this explains contemporary ideas that diversity matters more than intelligence or skill, and why intelligence is now seen to encompass emotional, visual and auditory intelligence. In the light of arguments in this chapter, supporters of therapeutic pedagogy also hope to counter invidious comparison.

Yet Sennet argues that recognising and valuing diversity will not make the problem of invidious comparison go away. Instead, developing a craft and taking part in the rituals associated with it protect people against invidious comparison, even if inequality remains a basic fact of human experience that we are always trying to make sense of. The notion of craft also enables public sector workers to resist the huge pressures on them that create feelings of helplessness and lead large numbers to quit. A view that professional work is a craft makes people feel genuinely useful and able to persevere under difficult conditions. Importantly for arguments in this chapter, Sennett argues that the craft of public service cannot thrive on pity, self-sacrifice or compassion.

An implication of these ideas is that education professionals cannot grant or confer esteem and respect: instead, both have to be earned. But another of his arguments is more controversial, namely that pro-fessionals dealing with people who suffer from poverty and lack of opportunity feel guilty about inequality and invidious comparison, particularly if they have themselves transcended these barriers through merit. The problem is that attempts to be genuinely useful and to meet clients' needs through empathy undermine autonomy:

> Autonomy is not simply an action; it requires also a relationship in which one party accepts that he or she cannot understand some-thing about the other. The acceptance that one cannot understand things about another gives both standing and equality in the relationship. Autonomy supposes at once connection and strange-ness, closeness and impersonality (2002: 79).

According to Sennett, modern welfare bureaucracies exclude this element of autonomy. In the light of arguments in this chapter, therapeutic pedagogy removes it completely. It is not easy to see how a therapeutic ethos creates the mutual respect that Freire saw as central to critical pedagogy. Nor can it encourage genuine craft and associated social rituals with it that are integral to mutual respect between professionals and their public (Sennett, 2002). Instead, therapeutic pedagogy offers the social rituals of an empathetic relationship founded on ideas that we are all frail, vulnerable and 'only human'. This appears to counter the impersonality of bureaucracies and the increasingly short-term, instrumental nature of many personal and professional transactions. Similarly, elevating empathy and emotional intelligence as the basis for educators' expertise appears to counter the increasing impersonality of many courses, or the difficulty of motivating students.

Conclusions

Therapeutic notions of low self-esteem, learners at risk or with fragile learning identities, now permeate policy and professional debates. Although it is crucial to define such notions and to understand what research tells us about their effects, it is perhaps more important to understand how they create a new sensibility that resonates with broader cultural pessimism about people's fragility and vulnerability. In turn, it is important to question whether therapeutic codes and symbols are seeping into pedagogy, thereby reinforcing or creating images of the 'diminished self' for professionals and students alike.

This chapter has aimed to show that preoccupation with self-esteem normalises a precarious psychological concept by extending it beyond a minority of people with mental health problems into mainstream life experience. Despite rhetoric to the contrary, optimism that education should enable people to transform their own and others' lives appears to be giving way to low expectations and introspection. In this context, social justice and liberal educational discourses about identity become infected with pessimistic images of vulnerability and human frailty, resonating with ideas about the 'diminished subject'. In turn, a more interventionist role for state agencies in private and public life, not as nanny but more subtly as therapist, makes it difficult to respect people deemed to be marginalised and vulnerable. If

Sennett is right, sympathy and empathy are easily transmogrified as condescension and then contempt (Sennett, 2003). Degraded compassion can never offer a basis for optimism or belief in the potential for human transformation and social progress.

Like the broader therapeutic ethos that sustains it, therapeutic pedagogy appears comforting and empowering. It also seems to resurrect lost voices in progressive and critical pedagogy. One implication of arguments in this chapter is that building people's self-esteem and exploring their identity suppress debates about what counts as useful curriculum content, or as empowering forms of learning for autonomy and equality, or about how communities can decide what types of education contribute to a meaningful life.

If these arguments are valid, they have serious implications for how we view each other and our students. Yet it is extremely difficult to challenge interest in self-esteem as an educational goal, especially amongst liberal and critical educators. For example, one response to criticisms of self-esteem as a legitimate educational concern is that they are offensive or uncaring, suggesting a crude 'stiff upper lip' view of resilience (see, for example, McGiveney, 2003). It is to be hoped that this chapter has shown the need to go beyond these objections by questioning the idea that therapeutic pedagogy is a new progressive voice in education. Arguments presented in this chapter offer a number of questions for getting beyond an emotive debate about whether rejection of self-esteem and therapeutic pedagogy shows an uncaring view of students. First, is there empirical evidence that concern about self-esteem and the rise of therapeutic pedagogy lead to the effects discussed here? Second, what are the practical and political purposes of exploring learners' and teachers' identity? While notions of identity can explain new oppressions and inequalities, do the cultural conditions outlined in this chapter lead merely to circular introspection, just like therapy itself, without any material and social consequences? Can a therapeutic identity be a basis for combating inequality? Third, can a debate about the purposes of critical pedagogy be resurrected without merely reverting to old, nostalgic ideas about social change?

Finally, a youth worker in an inner city London borough youth service wrote in response to my earlier paper that in stark contrast to a few years ago, his employers and colleagues now regard it as unprofessional to propose that young people deemed to be at risk should participate voluntarily in youth clubs and projects. According to him, youth workers' views about who is deemed to be at risk depend on class:

> If you are an affluent child, what you do with your time and your body is of little concern to the state. If you are poor, you lack the autonomy, rationality and responsibility to act on your own behalf. You are public property. This is where radical pedagogues will be drafted in by the youth services and education, looking to repair damaged identities, with a dose of cultural sensitivity that locates oppression in the lack of congruence between learner, institution and learning materials (Turner, 2003, personal communication).

Arguments in this chapter aim to offer a new voice of resistance to current directions in education policy and practice. They suggest that educators concerned about social justice and who believe in potential for self-determination and human agency face huge challenges. Nevertheless, two immediate responses are possible. One is to argue for education to offer genuine craft, knowledge and skills instead of offering a comforting therapy for groups or individuals perceived as fragile or vulnerable. The other is to resist calls to confer esteem upon people but rather to develop an optimistic sense of resilience and potential. This does not mean that teachers should avoid building confidence, supporting students or taking account of their feelings about education. But it does mean rejecting therapeutic pedagogy and the wider therapeutic ethos taking hold in education, because people's esteem, emotions and feelings are not a matter for state intervention, however benignly offered.

References

Ball, S (2000) Performance and fabrications in the education economy: towards the performative society, in: *Australian Educational Researcher*, 27, 2, 1-24

Ball, S (2003) The teacher's soul and the terrors of performativity, in: *Journal of Education Policy*, 8, 2, 215-228

Beck, U (1992) *Risk Society: Towards a New Modernity*. London: Sage

Blair, T (1997) Speech given at Stockwell Park School, Lambeth, December 1997

Bloomer, M (1997) *Curriculum making in post-16 education: the social conditions of studentship*. London: Routledge

Burn, E and Finnigan, T (2003) 'I've made it more academic by adding some snob words from the Thesaurus', in: Satterthwaite, J, Atkinson, E and Gale, K (eds) (2003) *Discourse, Power and Resistance: challenging the rhetoric of contemporary education*. London: Trentham Books

Campbell, D (2003) 'I wanted to quit but Victoria stopped me', in: *The Observer*, 31 August 2003, p3

Colley, H (2003) *Mentoring for social inclusion: a critical approach to nurturing mentor relationships*. London: Routledge Falmer

Colley, H and Hodkinson, P (2002) Problems with 'Bridging the Gap': the reversal of structure and agency in addressing social exclusion, in: *Critical Social Policy*, 21, 3, 337-361

Dale, R (1998) The State and governance of education, in: Halsey, A, Lauder, H, Brown, P Stuart-Wells, A (eds) (1998) *Education: culture, economy and society*. Oxford: Oxford University Press

DfES (2002a) Press release for 'Aim Higher' roadshows, 14 January 2002, www. DfES.gov.uk

DfES (2002b) *Transforming Youth Work*. London: DfES

Ecclestone, K (in press) Education or therapy?: the demoralisation of post-16 education, in: *British Journal of Educational Studies*, May 2004, volume etc to be confirmed

Edwards, R (2002) Mobilising lifelong learning: governmentality in educational practices, in: *Journal of Education Policy*, 17, 3, 353-365

Edwards, R and Nicoll, K (2001) Researching the Rhetoric of Lifelong Learning, in: *Journal of Education Policy*, 16, 2, 103-112

Emler, N (2001) *Self-esteem: the costs and causes of low self-worth*. York: Joseph Rowntree Foundation

Fevre, R (2001) *The Demoralisation of Western Culture: Social Theory and the Dilemmas of Modern Living*. London: Continuum

Giddens, A (1998) *Third way: the renewal of social democracy*. Oxford: Polity Press

Freire, P (1994) *Pedagogy of Hope: reliving 'Pedagogy of the Oppressed'*. New York: Continuum

Freire, P (1997) *Pedagogy of the Heart*. New York: Continuum

Freire, P (1999) *Pedagogy of the Oppressed – New revised 20th Anniversary edition*. New York: Continuum

Furedi, F (1999) *The Culture of Fear: Risk Taking and the Morality of Low Expectation*. London: Cassell

Furedi, F (2001) *Paranoid Parenting*. London: Penguin Books

Furedi, F (2002a) The Institutionalisation of Recognition: Evading the Moral Stalemate. Paper given to Demoralisation, Morality and Power Conference, University of Cardiff, 4-6 April 2002

Furedi, F (2002b) History has not yet begun. Paper given in a debate with Francis Fukuyama at the SpikedConference, After September 11th: Fear and Loathing in the West, 26 May 2002, Bishopsgate, London and at www.spiked-online.com

Furedi, F (2003) *Therapy Culture: creating vulnerability in an uncertain age*. London: Routledge

Gale, K (2003) Creative pedagogies of resistance in post-compulsory teacher education, in: Satterthwaite, J, Atkinson, E and Gale, K (eds) (2003) *Dis-*

course, Power and Resistance: challenging the rhetoric of contemporary education. London: Trentham Books

Giddens, A (1991) *Modernity and Self-identity: self and society in the late modern age.* Cambridge: Polity.

Harkin, J, Turner, G and Dawn, T (2001) *Teaching young adults: a handbook for teachers in post-compulsory education.* London: Routledge Falmer

Harrison, R, Clarke, J, Edwards, R and Reeve, F (2003) Power and resistance in further education: the discursive work of negotiating identities, in: Satterthwaite, J, Atkinson, E and Gale, K (eds) (2003) *Discourse, Power and Resistance: challenging the rhetoric of contemporary education.* London: Trentham Books

Hayes, D (2003) New Labour, New Professionalism, in Satterthwaite, J, Atkinson, E and Gale, K (eds) (2003) *Discourse, Power and Resistance: challenging the rhetoric of contemporary education.* London: Trentham Books

Hey, V (2003) Academia and working class femininities, in: *Gender and Education,* 15, 3, 319-335

James, K (2003) How low self-esteem affects adult learners, in: *Adults Learning,* 24, January 2003, 24-26

Jarvis, C (2001) Travellers' tales: from adult education to lifelong learning and beyond, in: *Studies in the Education of Adults,* 33, 2, 95-100

McGiveney, V (2003) Self-esteem is not psychobabble, in: FE Focus, *Times Educational Supplement,* 28 November, 2003, p26

Newman, T and Blackburn, S (2002) *Transitions in the Lives of Children and Young People: resilience factors.* Edinburgh: Barnardo's Policy Research and Influencing Unit/Scottish Executive

Nolan, J (1998) *The Therapeutic State: Justifying Government at Century's End.* New York: New York University Press

Patterson, L (2003) The three educational ideologies of the British Labour party, 1997-2001, in: *Oxford Review of Education,* 29, 2, 165-187

Preece, J (2001) Challenging the discourse of inclusion and exclusion with off-limits curricula, in: Gardner, J, Cairns, J and Lawton, D (eds.) *World Education Year Book: Values, Culture and Education.* London: Kogan Page

Pupavac, V (2001a) Therapeutic Governance: Psycho-social Intervention and Trauma Risk Management, in: *Disasters,* 25, 4, 358-372

Rogers, C (1961) *On Becoming a Person.* Boston: Houghton Mifflin

Rogers, C (1983) *Freedom to Learn for the 1980s,* New York: Merrill

Sarler, C (2003) No more heroes anymore, in: *The Observer* 31 August, 2003, p30

Sennett, R. (2002) *Respect: the formation of character in an age of inequality.* London: Allen Lane/Penguin

Social Exclusion Unit (1998) *Bridging the Gap: new opportunities for 16-18 year olds not in education or training.* London: HMSO

Sure Start (2002) Programme summary for Sure Start. Britwell-Northborough, (www. surestart.gov.uk)

9

Outsiders looking in or insiders looking out? Widening Participation in a post-1992 university

SANDRA SINFIELD, TOM BURNS AND DEBBIE HOLLEY

Sinfield, Burns and Holley analyse the Widening Participation agenda in terms of the power relations between management, lecturers and students. They take forward the analysis of trust offered by Avis, arguing that institutional trust is breaking down. The writers show that institutions tend to regulate ever more tightly the (transgressive) student through compulsory attendance at lectures and tutorials, compulsory core modules in this or that academic literacy based topic – all proposed in a bid to improve retention (and funding). What is being lost is the respect of the lecturer for the student and for the choices that they have made Whilst the Widening Participation agenda is related to debates around academic discourse, social class, employability and the skills agenda, the authors also look to the individual level where students are seen to be attempting to develop effective strategies to negotiate a hostile and threatening academic environment. The voices of the students interviewed here resonate with those in the next chapter of Evans and Martin's student teachers as they struggle to reconstruct their identities as learners in Higher Education establishments.

Introduction

Widening Participation (WP) is flagged up as the next big thing in the government's education, education, education juggernaut, with the goal of 50% of 18-30 year olds in or through Higher Education (HE) by 2010. This paper explores Widening Participation in relation to changes in the power relationships between management, lecturers and students. With a focus on new managerialism, Widening Participation is related to wider debates about academic discourse, social class, employability and the skills agenda. Drawing on informal interviews with students accessing Learning Development in drop-in support workshops and in HE Orientation modules, the experiences and perceptions of the Widening Participation student are considered as we explore the position of the new student in a new university.

The rise of new managerialism

In 1979, Margaret Thatcher and the Conservative Party were swept into power on an election slogan of 'rolling back the frontiers of state'. The economy was to be transformed, and the argument was that the policies forged would address Britain's problems of rising inflation and deteriorating international competitiveness. By the late 1980s, Britain consequently experienced a programme of deregulation, privatisation and tax cuts. The reduction of public spending complemented Thatcher's attachment to free markets, greater choice and rampant individualism (Hutton, 1995). These policies were to change the top-down, monolithic organisations of the Keynesian welfare state and alter the nature of public sector management. In parallel, there was a trend toward the decentralisation of health, housing and education. Simultaneously, important areas such as regional policymaking and the role of the Metropolitan Boroughs, were centralised. Pollitt *et al* (1998) explain that it is perfectly possible to decentralise or devolve authority over certain issues while simultaneously centralising authority over others. This led to the paradox that whilst extensive decentralisation took place, it appears that from the 1980s the UK became one of the most centralised states in Europe.

The right to manage

The introduction of managerialism within the public sector became a central strategy, representing a movement away from traditional bureaucratic paternalism (Pollitt, 1990). Two varieties of managerialism have been identified. The first is described as Neo-Taylorism, which focuses on obtaining more for less. The second, the excellence school, derives from the work of Peters (1989) and combines quality, corporate commitment, closeness to the customer and entrepreneurialism. For Pollitt (1993), managerialism meant that overall control by managers was both necessary and desirable.

Rather than regarding these two varieties of managerialism as separate, Newman and Clarke (1994) suggest that they should be seen as integrated, and show how this new managerialism stresses the 'right to manage'. This reflects other changes in the public sector initiated by the government, such as concern about the economic costs of welfare, a dependency culture, and the power of bureaucrats and professionals. Arguably, the last of these was the government's main concern. 'Arrogant' professionals were arraigned alongside 'inflexible' bureaucrats and 'interfering' local politicians, all of whom had prevented efficient, effective and economic public services. They argue that the only way to disentangle and defuse these 'interlocking modes of power' is by the combination of markets and management.

It is here that emergent forms of managerialism, with all the implications for the content and organisation of professional work, specifically the work of lecturers, become important with relationships between professionals and managers constituted unevenly between and within different organisations.

Managing Higher Education

New managerialism is justified, especially in the popular press, as a rational solution to calls for greater efficiency and public accountability. In particular, it has led to the increased use of performance management as a tool for setting and monitoring goals. This approach is often simplified as, 'what gets measured gets done', a simplification which captures the dynamic, objective and transparent philosophy of the paradigm. However, new managerialism remains problematic: it is frequently attacked through the corollary of the simplification, which is that what does not get measured gets neglected (Blalock, 1999).

Until recently, it might have been argued that Higher Education has maintained a degree of academic autonomy, particularly when compared to the centralist thrust that has been described in schools (Fergusson, 1994). However, the use of central funding to promote a competitive and expansionist market in Further and Higher Education radically altered the culture of management in many institutions.

This so-called agenda of modernisation for Higher Education could be seen as being part of a wider debate around performance and quality. Performance indicators have provided management with both a technology and a 'rational' justification for exerting increased bureaucratic control (Kirkpatrick and Lucio, 1995).

This is particularly problematic given the complex nature of education, and the argument that many measures are superficial and over-simplistic and that the choice of measures to be employed is often made by management, or at the least, passed on from funding councils via management. This has left some lecturers feeling that the most important elements of their work must now be neglected in order to demonstrate that less important, but more visible measures have been met.

HE might need to examine how this has been implemented in FE, as FE is already adjusting to the influx of the new and even the new, new student who is typically younger and more disenfranchised than, say, the Access students of old. Whereas previously students were encouraged into FE colleges to experience a more mature teaching and learning environment, now the emphasis has shifted to the visible ways that the FE lecturer manages the new FE student. This has meant an insistence on the lecturer, prior to meeting students and assessing their wants and needs (Rogers, 1994), producing rigid lessons plans and Schemes of Work. Pedagogic practice, rather than evolving, has moved towards spoon feeding, coupled with an authoritarian emphasis on punctuality and attendance, which is monitored by extensive paperwork and liaison with student mentors, personal tutors, Programme Area Leaders, Heads of School, parents, Work Placement Co-ordinators and Business. Not only is this what was typically tried *and failed* at school with these students, it leaves no space to build trust relationships with the new student. It also allows no time to evolve strategies more akin to education, that might actually work with the new FE students to help them develop their emergent student identities (Holmes, 2001). What you have are implicitly transgressive students classically managed by implicitly transgressive staff.

The strategic management of pedagogy

Further governmental policies that were intended to enhance the quality of Higher Education have added to the process of top-down management described above. In particular, pedagogy, once purely the concern of the academics directly involved in course delivery, has now become an issue for strategy. The Higher Education Funding Council for England (HEFCE) has linked elements of University funding to the creation and implementation of Teaching and Learning Strategies. Consequently, in many institutions pedagogy has been placed in the hands of strategic management for the first time.

Moreover, with the choice of pedagogic approach being a matter of strategy rather than tactics, the lecturers' primary tool (pedagogic approaches) for coping with the current push for Mass HE and Widening Participation, and the resulting increase in student diversity and numbers, is being taken out of their control. Although some degree of latitude does remain, the choice of teaching techniques is becoming constrained by the decisions of senior management. In line with other trends towards centralisation, the establishment of such strategies seems likely to promote further conformity in order to establish common standards.

David Noble (2002:3) argues that this negative discourse is further exacerbated by the increasing commodification of education *per se*: the educational experience has been disintegrated and distilled into 'discrete, reified, and ultimately saleable things or packages of things.' The first step in this process is the assemblage of the course into packages: learning outcomes, syllabi, lectures, lessons, exams. These commodities barely reflect what actually takes place in the educational experience, and 'lend an illusion of order and predictability to an undetermined process' (*op cit*). Subsequent steps include the removal of these items from their producers, the teachers, so that they are given an independent existence, apart from the creator. This constitutes the alienation of ownership as control of course material is surrendered. The final step is the assembled course sale in the market place, at a profit, where the market, not the creator determines its worth. Thus teachers become producers, students become consumers and their relationship takes on not 'education', but a shadow of education, 'an assemblance of pieces without the whole.' (Noble,

2002; 4). It is in this atmosphere of commodification and top-down micro-management that Widening Participation is lodged.

Widening Participation – who is it for?

Margaret Hodge (Minister for Lifelong Learning, 2002-03) has placed Widening Participation in the context of New Labour harmonising the previous left wing agenda when out of office, focusing on equality and social justice, to a far more centre right policy once elected. This has emphasised the role of education in fostering economic prosperity. Hodge has acknowledged the tension between these two competing objectives in education policy and offered New Labour's third way: prosperity needs social inclusion, with the talents of all being developed. At the same time she has asserted that not all graduates would be able to take up what we would call 'graduate jobs', whilst they might still have incurred graduate debts. Her various speeches and reported comments in the press barely mask an eugenicist agenda, with elite Higher Education for some, and an inferior, vocational HE for the masses. (Hodge, 2002)

Widening Participation – decreased funding – poorly targeted

Whilst both Conservative and Labour governments have expressed a desire for a more inclusive Higher Education system, Leathwood (2003) indicates that British Governments have begun to systematically reduce the unit of resource available to Higher Education: from 1976-86 funding was reduced by 29%, with a further reduction of 38% by 1999. Thus class sizes rose and staff/student ratios worsened as young people from a wide range of educational backgrounds began to enter Universities and mixed ability teaching became increasingly common (Bennett, 2002).

As government commitments to Widening Participation have not been fully funded, it has also been argued that they have not been accurately targeted. Specifically, the National Audit Office flagged up concerns re targeting of funds in their report, which showed that of £77 million available to improve access, most went to middle-class graduates returning to Higher Education, instead of working-class first timers (NAO, 2001). The recent Government White Paper, outlining its policy on a more inclusive agenda, does not take account of research carried out into working-class students and their needs and perceptions of entry into Higher Education. A recent report (Archer *et al*, 2003) from London Metropolitan University outlines the disaster that the White Paper, if implemented, would be for a social inclusion agenda.

Widening Participation – it's a struggle

Anie (2001) in an employability study looking at employment outcomes of students in a new university and Leathwood (2003) in a longitudinal study following 600 students enrolled at a new university – from 1999 to 2002 both write of the 'struggles' faced by the Widening Participation student. These struggles are various and inter locking, with cumulative negative effects felt particularly by those students from groups previously excluded from Higher Education as they negotiate HE in this new, cold climate. Typically the WP student, in a post-92 university, struggles to adjust to the occult demands of HE, a struggle made worse by the negative stereotypes that the university and the wider society have of them. This new student struggles to study full time whilst working in one or two part time jobs in an effort to support themselves and their families. This is hard enough in itself and these students are very aware that this additional workload damages their grades. Pushed to seek employment rather than following up postgraduate study, the non-traditional student understands that they are least likely to get the graduate job that will allow them to fight their way out of the financial crisis within which HE has placed them:

> Working-class students recognise that cheaper degrees from new universities are worth less in the job market, but they are restricted to studying there because they are unwilling to take on large debts. (Archer 18/01/02)

Financial hardship represents a struggle misrepresented by Hodge when Minister for Lifelong Learning. In a *Times Higher* article on student debt (*Times Higher Educational Supplement*, 7th Feb 2003), Hodge is reported as saying: 'What is it legitimate to subsidise? Are mobile phones a legitimate cost which if not met through student support will prevent working-class kids from going to university?' She went on: 'Low-paid work is a good life experience for a pretty privileged bunch of young people.' In these utterances Hodge perhaps exemplifies the problem. Her lack of awareness of the real pain and struggle of the previously disenfranchised as they negotiate HE expressly ignores reduced funding and incremental fees and only serves to reinforce the myth of meritocracy. Further, in linking Widening Participation and working-class access to mobile phones (icons of the lumpen proletariat), Hodge works to obscure the problematic nature of education and its role in maintaining and reinforcing the unequal power relations in our 'classless' society. As Tett, citing Bourdieu and Passeron, puts it: 'Education could be 'the royal road to the democratisation of culture if it did not consecrate the initial cultural inequalities by ignoring them" (Tett, 2000: 190). For our students low paid jobs are a way of life, not an exotic life enhancing experience.

Retention

Retention statistics are often used against the new universities that do attempt to embrace the Widening Participation student; typically such institutions will appear to have poor retention statistics. However, whilst over 30% of the students in the Leathwood longitudinal study were shown to have dropped out after three years, many students are not retention casualties, but rather reflect what a blunt measuring instrument this is. Students may be excluded temporarily for non-payment of fees, others intermit whilst not knowing the technical term, still others will leave full time study, but continue as part time students. Negative retention statistics often mask heroic struggles for success.

Coming in from the cold – the outsiders looking in

Our University has a Widening Participation brief and actively recruits those who are deemed non-traditional students. This is not an homogenous group but consists of those previously excluded from or not encouraged into HE, including those from our local working-class and ethnic minority communities and English speakers of other languages. The QAA Subject Review for Business (2002) noted that just 12% of students entered at 18 with the typical A' level profile: the rest were classified as mature. 74% of our students had no previous family member through HE and 60% did not pay fees. Further, many of our students speak of painful educational experiences at school and the majority suffer low self-esteem and self-confidence. Leathwood (2003) notes that this continual feeling of not being 'good enough' relates to 'systems of oppression' within society rather than individual traits or personality failings and constitutes further evidence of the struggle faced by non-traditional students: a struggle typically not considered via the strategic management of pedagogy.

The authors, as with Anie (2001) and Leathwood (2003) above, have a particular interest in the non-traditional student in the non-traditional university and the student experiences noted below are drawn from informal interviews we have had with students over the last four years. We have particularly focused on students in what are now termed HE Orientation Modules and on students accessing Learning Development support.[1]

Outsiders coming in

Since the sixties there have been calls for more people to enter HE to foster economic prosperity and indeed self-development and improvement and financial reward have all been offered as reasons for entering HE:

- I wanted to follow up, not just be a nursery nurse, I wanted more

- Bring myself up to speed and see if I had a brain

- I'm at the top of my scale, I'm earning less than the people around me [teachers]...and I can't go any further

These goals did seem to change as students moved through their programmes of study and many students reported that they felt changed by their experiences. Comments below are taken from a small sample of informal interviews conducted with mature women juggling family, work in Early Years and part time study on the open-entry Early Childhood Study Scheme:

- I feel it's part of my life now

- You feel so special. You really feel marvellous. You think, gosh, I can be clever again. It's a good, a good feeling

- No, no. My reason is now for myself and to try and change things

- I wanted to do more. I want to have my ideas...I want to be on top

Thus, despite the falling unit and poor targeting of resources, despite Hodge relegating the majority of students to educational backwaters and implicitly less respected vocational degrees, our students, as Giddens (1996) might argue, are embracing risk, engaging in the modernisation project and re-writing their life narratives through educational struggle.

Outsiders settling in

> Those triumphalist celebrations of fluidity always overlook the fact that being unfixed, mobile, in-between, can distress as much as it liberates. So [that one's] sense of class identity is uncertain, torn and oscillating – caught on a cultural cusp. (Medhurst in Munt, 2000: 20)

Becoming a student was a very emotionally charged activity for all the students we interviewed. Whilst there was a sense of anticipation and excitement, the over riding emotional experience was of fear and anxiety. Common words to describe initial experiences are apprehensive, het-up, nervous, nerve racking, inadequate, frightened and terrified:

- The first day I came into Business Skills – it was terrifying. I thought that all those people were looking at me coming through the door. My lecturer later told me there had been 330 people there – that's more than the whole of our sixth form (Student A, on a Business Orientation Module)

- The words just seem to swim past me and I can't understand what is going on (Student B, on a Business Orientation Module)

Early Childhood Studies Students:

- I thought they were all looking at me and thinking what is that old woman doing here

- I was glad but scared. I thought you stupid idiot, why didn't you leave things as they were?

- Why, why, why couldn't you be happy just going to work?

Fear and a lack of self-confidence have a real impact on the quality of the student learning experience, and affect that learning:

- But that week when you did that ... I hated that and I was really uncomfortable the whole lesson... I was so unsure and not confident... I thought I don't know what the hell she wants me to do.

And you know as soon as you're in that position you can't learn anything, you can't take anything in... and it was awful. It was horrible. I didn't like that at all. I found that really hard.

The unequal power relations of educational discourse can very easily reinforce the negative self-perceptions of students, as can lecturers, perhaps, who see themselves primarily as academics (keepers of the academy), rather than as educators. This is further exacerbated when students are non-traditional and is perhaps *felt* even more keenly by the mature student who has previously experienced the world in powerful ways and who now feels powerless in a middle-class environment:

> 'class is felt, class wounds, class hurts and those ... on a cusp between classes bruise particularly easily' (Medhurst in Munt, 2000: 21).

Leathwood argues that the negative feelings experienced by our students are not individual character flaws but are emblematic of the injustices inherent in an unequal society, which are then replicated in our unequal education system and its management practices. Alarmingly, the Widening Participation agenda itself can become part of the problem when, as with Hodge, it seems to define the non-traditional student only in negative terms. Moreover, with recruitment policy, retention strategy and pedagogical practice the business of management and being monitored by appraisals, targets and performance indicators, seems to be moving away from education and more towards the regulation of desire (Lillis, 2001).

Insiders looking out – attitudes to our students

The Widening Participation student is vilified in the popular press and the Houses of Commons and Lords; Burn, 2003, hooks, 1994, Leathwood, 2003, Lillis, 2001, Luttrell, 1997, Medhurst, 2000, and Reay, 1998 record responses towards these students that are classed, raced, gendered and aged. Rather than celebrating the phenomenon of Widening Participation, the non-traditional student is pathologised and disparaged. Burn (2003) writes of how non-traditional *staff* and students are humiliated and silenced in the academic environment; a response perhaps captured by Starkey: 'There are Mickey Mouse students for whom Mickey Mouse degrees are quite appropriate'.

Lillis (2001) specifically links current and continual debates about the 'crisis' in education and the preoccupation with 'skills' and 'standards' to the reaction to Widening Participation. She critiques HE for not adopting a broader frame of reference to the contexts of its participants and to its own practices:

> Student language is made visible and problematised but the language of discourse and the pedagogical practices in which they are embedded usually remain invisible, taken as 'given'. (Lillis, 2001: 22)

Whilst Lillis warns that the skills agenda is itself disabling of the non-traditional student, many of our senior staff warn that we are actually harsher towards our students: 'I think we give them too many opportunities to fail...' 'I'm an external examiner for other institutions and I know that we are harsher here.' So a key problem for the non-traditional student is not only the academic environment, and the ways that students perceive themselves and are themselves perceived within that academic context; but that in the race to maintain 'standards' the non-traditional student in a non-traditional university is actually treated more harshly than the traditional student at a high status university.

At the same time many tutors at our university report their enthusiasm for our students. Lecturers who value working with non-traditional students anecdotally report that the teaching and learning process is itself facilitated by the interest and motivation of the students. Typically the adult student wants to embrace the risk and engage in the struggle of Higher Education; there is a desire to understand the subject, *de facto*, to engage with epistemology and the contested nature of knowledge claims. Typically our students are interested in active, reflective and creative learning strategies that facilitate learning and studying (Burns and Sinfield, 2003). This interest and engagement is fostered when we in HE make transparent and problematic the forms and processes of education itself (Lillis, 2001) and remember to trust the student. All tutors and particularly 'once-working-class academics' need to:

> remember their own pasts, and let their working-class students reach their own accommodation with discourses of belonging, identity and power (Medhurst in Munt, 2000: 31).

Conclusions
New managerialism and the development of pedagogy

Traditionally lecturers have enjoyed considerable autonomy in their approach to teaching, with pedagogy viewed as part of the remit of domain experts. However, recent years have seen ongoing governmental intervention, including widening participation in HE. In addition to the introduction of teaching and learning strategies, the government has sought to justify its policies with pedagogic recommendations for universities.

Pedagogical development is not new; what is new is the change in the locus of control for this evolutionary process. Whilst earlier developments were driven by educational and psychological research, recent changes have been instigated through government policy. This has resulted in the agenda for professional development and practice becoming the concern of Senior Management, as opposed to lecturers or professional developers with background and expertise in these areas. The trend has been to move pedagogy out of the domain of professionalism and into the realm of policy. The reality is that pedagogy has been placed in the hands of management, via funding bodies, for the first time.

Further, with Senior Management assuming the 'right to manage' recruitment, retention and learning and teaching strategies, what results potentially ignores the complexity of education and offers not quality and closeness, but a system that works to regulate implicitly deficit and transgressive staff and students.

The outsiders looking in – what do they see?

They see Margaret Hodge linking accessibility and employment, with a huge caveat:

> Research shows that eight out of ten new jobs created in the next decade... will need the skills and knowledge from HE – but not necessarily the 'academic degree' (Hodge, 2002).

Many working class students will never enter HE for fear of debt (Archer 18.01.02); of those who do take the risk, our tutors argue that they have already been failed by the education system. Pathologised by policy makers, the keepers of the academy and influential others, Widening Participation students are neither failures nor remedial but they are engaged in painful and often debilitating 'struggle' (Leathwood, 2003). Lillis (2001) links the ongoing debates about the 'crisis' in education to a negative reaction towards the move to ever wider participation. The Widening Participation student, rather than being part of diluting or weakening HE, is often more harshly assessed than students in the old universities.

Ironically, rather than the middle-class institution that is HE, it is the Widening Participation student, scapegoated and vilified in the Lords and the popular press and humiliated and silenced in the academic environment itself, who is engaged in the risky and costly modernisation process. Many of us acknowledge that the success of much of our teaching is due to the diversity of our student body and the high levels of motivation, commitment and enthusiasm that the students themselves bring to the university. At the same time, it is an opportune moment to examine our own practices, rather than problematising the practices of our students. We do need to make transparent the forms and processes of academic discourse and work to facilitate student negotiation of the potentially hostile environment that is academia (Burns and Sinfield, 2003).

Note

1   **HE Orientation modules** typically consist of intensive programmes that introduce students to – and rehearse them in – the various forms, practices and strategies necessary for academic success. Such programmes may or may not include an element of deconstructing the discourse and power relations of HE. They may or may not include some form of introduction to the 'cultural capital' typically required of successful graduates. **Learning Development** is sometimes known as Learning or Study Support or Study and Academic Development. Previously known as Study Skills, this term is falling out of favour as linked to a deficit notion of the student and a 'fixing it' notion of learning development. Learning Development is an area of HE that is currently very dynamic. The whole WP debate has alerted many HE practitioners to the ingress of perhaps less academically inducted students and the discussion around Learning Development is whether or not to remediate these students – or to empower them.

Bibliography

Anie, A (2001) *Widening Participation – Graduate Employability Project* University of North London (now London Metropolitan University)

Archer, L (2002) Access Elite, in *Times Higher Education Supplement* 18/01/02

Archer, L Hutchings, H and Ross, A (2003) *Higher Education and social class.* London and New York: Routledge Farmer

Bennett, R (2002) *Lecturers attitudes to new teaching methods* London Guildhall University, International Journal of Management Education

Blalock, A (1999) Evaluation Research and the Performance Management Movement: From Estrangement to Useful Integration? *Evaluation*, 5, 2, 117-149.

Bourdieu, P and Passeron, J-C (1979) *Reproduction in Education, Society and Culture*. London: Sage

Burn, E and Finnigan, T (2002) I've made it more academic by adding some snob words from the thesaurus. Conference paper, Discourse Power Resistance in post-compulsory education and training, University of Plymouth, April 2002

Burns, T and Sinfield, S (2003) *Essential Study Skills: the complete guide to success @ university*. London: Sage

Clarke, K 20 May 1991 (*Hansard* 1991)

Fergusson (1994) Managerialism in Education, in: Clarke, C, Cochrane, A and McLaughlin, E (eds) *Managing Social Policy*. London: Sage

Giddens, A (1996) *Consequences of Modernity*. Cambridge: Pollitty Press

Hodge, M, Secretary of State for Education (2002) Keynote speech What is College and University education for? Church House Westminster; Education Conference 24/01/02

Hodge, M (2003) in Saunders, C 'Fact: term jobs damage grades', in *Times Higher Education Supplement* 07.02.03

Holmes, L www.re-skills.org.uk/thesis/ February 2002 (See also: www.re-skill. org.uk;www.graduate-employability.org.uk; www.odysseygroup. org.uk)

hooks, b (1994) *Teaching to Transgress*. London: Routledge

Hutton, W (1995) *The State We're In*. London: Cape

Kirkpatrick, I and Lucio, M (1995) *The Politics of Quality in the Public sector*. London: Routledge

Leathwood, C and O'Connell, P (2002) 'It's a struggle': the construction of the 'new student' in higher education in Institute for Policy Studies in Education, London Metropolitan University (Presented to the SRHE Annual Conference 10-12 December 2002, University of Glasgow)

Lillis, T (2001) *Student Writing, Access, Regulation, Desire*. London: Routledge

Luttrell, W (1997) *Schoolsmart and Motherwise*. London: Routledge

Medhurst, A (2000) If Anywhere: Class Identifications and Cultural Studies Academics, in: Munt, S (Ed) *Cultural Studies and the Working Class*. London: Cassell

Munt, S (Ed) (2000) *Cultural Studies and the Working Class*. London: Cassell

National Audit Office (2001) *Widening participation in Higher Education in England*

Newman, J and Clarke, J (1994) Going about our business? The managerialism of public services, in: Clarke, C, Cochrane, A and McLaughlin, E (eds) *Managing social Policy*. London; Sage

Noble, D (2002) *Digital Diploma Mills: The automation of Higher Education*. New York: Monthly Review Press

Pollitt, C, Birchall, J and Putman, K (1998) *Decentralising Public Service Management*. London: Macmillan Press

QAA (2002) *Subject Review for Business* (London Metropolitan University)

Reay, D (1998) *Class Work*. London: UCL Press

Rogers, C (1994) *Upper Saddle River* NJ: Merrill

Tett, L (2000) I'm Working Class and Proud of It – gendered experiences of non-traditional participants in higher education, in *Gender and Education*, 1(2): 183 – 194

10

Widening Participation and studentship in HE: learner perspectives and reflections: the impact of discourse

JULIE EVANS AND WENDY MARTIN

Julie Evans and Wendy Martin argue that although the Widening Participation agenda has brought into Higher Education large numbers of non-traditional students, many of these students bring with them a range of insecurities related to their past educational experience which are exacerbated by the traditional discourses they encounter there. Evans and Martin turn to Bourdieu and Harré to provide a conceptual basis for the data collected from a series of interviews with student teachers entering Higher Education. The chapter examines specifically the uneasy negotiations between the roles of student, student-teacher and lecturer. Students' strategies of discursive resistance are examined and developed further in the detailed case study offered by Haggis in the concluding chapter.

This chapter discusses a small scale research study in the Faculty of Arts and Education (now the Faculty of Education) at the University of Plymouth, undertaken in Autumn 2001. The research involved a group of mature students in the early stages of either a Postgraduate Certificate in Education (Post Compulsory Education and Training) [PGCE-PCET] or Certificate in Education (Post Compulsory Education and Training) [Cert. Ed.-PCET]. Teaching experience varied widely, and participants ranged in educational experience from those with no entry qualifications to postgraduates. The presence of students with little or no entry qualifications on a Higher Education (HE) programme can be seen to be largely connected to the Widening Participation (WP) programme which has been evident in UK education since the late 1980s.

The chapter focuses on the discourses, power relations and resistances that were occurring within a group of PCET student teachers. The aim is to offer an insight into the initial experiences of what could be described as non-traditional students, that is those whose entry might be seen to be resulting from the Widening Participation agenda. We will draw upon Bourdieu's notion of *habitus* as a means of understanding some of the power and resistance that permeated through many students' early experiences of HE, and on Harré's (1998) conceptualisation of the 'knower' and the 'known' to explore both power relations and identities. We also draw on Weil's (1989) concept of disjunction to further explore personal and social identities. We suggest that many students who have had negative experiences of formal education in their younger lives, twenty (or even thirty) years later find themselves operating within those same educational discourses, and are once again internalising their anxieties as 'personal failure.' As Reay *et al* found in their study of mature students' transition to HE:

> '...all assume a rhetoric of personal inadequacy to explain events invariably linked to processes and structures beyond their personal control.' (2002:16).

The issue of widening participation within HE has been well documented over recent years with targets of increased participation within HE being set at 50% of 18-30 year olds (DFES, 2003). Archer *et al*. (2003) rightly question whether, if this target is met, social inclusion and social justice have been achieved? Older students and non-traditional entry students have been significant beneficiaries of policies of Widening Participation in HE and growth in HE provision (Connor *et al*, 1999). However, much of the work surrounding the WP agenda has focused on the educational trajectories of the 16-19 age group, and although not always explicitly stated, much of what is written has a sub-text based on the definition of a mature student as being anyone over the age of 21. This fails to fully encompass the diversity of age ranges, life experiences and lifestyles of the group of students who come under the umbrella of the term 'mature students.' Additionally much of the data focuses on students who are in full-time education, studying on a three or four year traditional degree programme. The transition into HE of students studying on a part-time basis combined with paid employment, or who are studying for the first time at certificate or diploma level seems, thus far, to have lacked in depth study. Reay *et al.* (2001, 2002a, 2002b), however, have started to rectify this imbalance, and their work has put the classed, racialised and gendered aspects of re-entry into education firmly at the heart of both sociological and educational debate.

Methodology

The research project grew from discussions between a tutor and a group of students who found that academic jargon was impacting on the students' learning. The tutor felt that density in the style of academic writing and the use of long words in many education books was perhaps an unnecessary *impasse* that many students were having difficulty with (Satterthwaite, 2003). This block seemed to act as a conduit for resistance so that students were disengaging with the reading in the early part of the programme. Initially the students were asked one question: 'what is it that gets in the way of your learning?' Sixteen students were interviewed either individually or in small self-selected groups.

The interviews took place between six to eight weeks into the Cert. Ed./PGCE programme, involving both full-time and part-time students. The students were at the stage when a range of ideas had been deconstructed, leaving some of them feeling a range of in-securities. For some, the euphoria associated with having completed their City and Guilds 7307 certificate[1] had been replaced with a new set of anxieties. As we will see later many of the students had internalised these anxieties and questioned whether this next step in their educational journey was a step too far, or whether they were simply 'not teacher material.'

Mature students and the Widening Participation agenda

The WP agenda has, arguably, been an attempt to compensate for the earlier failings of the state school system, focusing on students who underachieved at school. According to Wagner (2000), one of the greatest achievements of WP was the opening of HE to non-traditional students in the 1980s and 1990s, thereby attracting mature students. However, we would argue that whilst the opening of HE has been emancipatory for many class, gender and ethnic minority groups, the position of mature students has not been as clear as much of the literature, and indeed policy documents, implies.

According to the Department for Education and the Environment (DfEE, now the Department for Education and Skills (DfES)), the number of graduate students who entered as mature students rose from approximately 10% in the 1980s to 30% in the 1990s (cited in Reay *et al.*, 2002). Woodley and Wilson (2002) state that by the 1980s mature students accounted for over half of all new entrants to HE, with that figure set to rise even further. Whilst we have already seen a significant growth in opportunities for mature students, the mature student population is heavily skewed to the lower end of the age range and according to Woodley and Wilson (2002) could be better defined as delayed school leavers. Indeed, for the under-30 year old age group, the government has set a target of increasing participation in HE to 50% by 2010 (DfES, 2003).

Previous studies of students' entry into Higher Education have focused on the identity shifts of the learner (Green and Webb, 1997), and the personal meaning of becoming an adult learner in HE (Davies and Williams, 2001). Davies and Williams argue that for many mature students the move from 'non-participant' in education to 'student' constitutes a particular challenge to previous identities. This may become a point of conflict in terms of students' own experiences of their teaching practice, and in particular NVQ-style[2] assessment methodologies, compared with what they experience as learners within the HE environment. This makes their experiences of transition significantly different from many other student groups: as well as the educational/learning factors, issues of developing professional identities associated with teaching are intertwined with their role as learners in the university environment.

Concomitant to the drive towards increasing student numbers, educational and career aspirations have become embedded in a discourse in which participation in Further and Higher Education is constructed as offering the individual greater determination over career paths and the use of their labour power, thus providing increased possibilities for self-realisation (Avis, 1998:5 cited in Warrington, 2003:96/97). Associated with this opening up of HE to mature students is the increasing need to go through a process of credentialisation, or what Woodley and Wilson (2002) call credentialism, by which employees need to be updating their skills and formalising their occupational competence by gaining nationally recognised qualifications.

WP and the credentialisation process are further impacted upon locally by our peninsular location and the limited geographical access to HE. Many students do not have the choice of universities and courses which has been suggested as a factor in students' transition (see Reay *et al.*, 2001). Thus the picture in this region is blurred by the limited nature of access to HE..

The opening up of HE to non-traditional entrants, as a result of policies such as Widening Participation, has undoubtedly offered greater numbers of women, people from working-class backgrounds and ethnic minorities an opportunity to re-engage with education. For these groups, entry into HE is access to something that has been previously denied. Whilst the route through GCSEs, A levels[3] and on to university is a natural progression for many middle class young people, the trajectory for working-class individuals, and certain mature students, is much less clear cut. Opening up HE is only part of a process and many students face other battles once they return. One of the 'battlegrounds' is often where the unconscious is clashing with the conscious, in that many students who have consciously de-cided to pursue further study face internal dilemmas regarding their positioning or role within the academy. As stated above, this may particularly apply to students who are concurrently teachers. A useful framework for analysing these dilemmas is the work of Pierre Bourdieu.

Bourdieu's (1977) conceptualisation of the *habitus* is as a schema that classifies rules and expectations and then unconsciously directs individuals to make certain choices. Our habitus is inculcated as much by experience as by explicit teaching. According to Jenkins (1992) it is the mediating link between the subjective world of the individual, and the cultural world which that individual shares with others. Similar to Weber's notion of life chances, our *habitus* is built around our early experiences and our socialisation structures, which then becomes our internal 'software system,' used to guide interaction within wider social structures. This interaction then relates to subsequent perceptions and aspirations. It becomes, according to Swartz (1997), a matrix that generates self-fulfilling prophecies according to different class opportunities. Importantly for this discussion, structural disadvantage can be internalised and produce self-defeating behaviours. Bourdieu asserts that the *habitus* 'leads individuals into a kind of submission to order' (cited in Swartz, 1997:105), which arguably legitimates economic and social inequality by concealing structural advantages amongst the *milieu* of a perceived meritocracy.

Bourdieu's argument shows that for many mature students, and particularly those whose access is associated with WP, re-engagement with the education system, although a conscious decision, actually generates the negative experiences and labelling of their place in the educational order. Nash (1990) argues that *habitus* gains its history and generates its practices for some time, even when the objective conditions which gave rise to it have disappeared. Bourdieu's notion of *habitus* is clearly visible in the students' comments.

Competing Discourses

Before exploring the concept of *habitus* further, it is worth pausing to examine the competing discourses which emerged from the data. These included: the conceptualisation of 'adult learners', their occupational identities, the roles of 'teacher' and 'lecturer', the peer group, and increasing credentialsation, particularly as this latter related to progressing through the perceived system from City and Guilds 7307 to Cert Ed/PGCE. For some students this was not just about occupational mobility, but also about personal development and self-emancipation.

Fear and resistance amongst the course participants was palpable at the time the interviews took place, and this can be directly linked to the WP agenda. As Daloz (1990) suggests school (or college/university) is often a reminder of a former failure due to a whole range of factors, which has resulted in an educational script of significant fear and resistance. Fear and resistance are likely to be heightened when non-traditional entrants have had negative early education experiences.[4]

Mann (2001) argues that in entering HE students encounter a pre-existing discourse where they are positioned in different ways and where they are estranged from the language and the culture. This may, according to Mann, provoke feelings of estrangement, disorientation, voicelessness and ineffectualness which we experience when we are foreigners in a strange land. Many students certainly expressed feelings that support Mann's analysis. For example, the specialised language and terminology used by tutors and authors was mentioned in all interviews and the students' consternation with this coincided with the very early stages of their learning on the programme. For all the students interviewed both specialised language and jargon were huge barriers which were preventing them from breaking through their initial fears. The literature was all too often clouded by words that read like a foreign language, which was inadvertently silencing students even further.

Weil (1989) offers a notion of disjunction which she describes as 'feeling at odds with oneself...disjunction can be associated with feelings of alienation, anger, frustration and confusion' (p161). Disjuncture is also associated with who we are, so it is about personal and social identities. Weil argues that the possibilities can be significantly heightened when some of the sources of that disjuncture remain invisible, as Caitlin's questioning indicates:

> 'I go to bed thinking about what I'm reading and I mean it might all turn out to be nothing at the end of the day just all these thoughts... so all these thoughts that I've had for all these years which I thought were cut and dried now all these thoughts can be broken down. It depends which hilltop you are on as to what you see... all these thoughts are very confusing nothing is tangible. At the end of the day if you listen to Jeff (the tutor) it might all amount to nothing.

Additionally, intriguing questions were raised about how these student teachers position themselves as learners, and what happens to their confidence when they move between the roles of 'teacher' and 'learner.'

Evidence of dislocation of *habitus* and disjuncture was striking amongst students who had entered the Certificate in Education course after completing the City and Guilds 7307, so that they were familiar with some of the terminology. They commented that this course appeared to be much harder, and that they were having difficulties in breaking down the language and jargon barriers. Students appeared to be struggling with both the philosophical questions of the fundamental purposes of education and the social aspects of being a student. This is reminiscent of the work of Harré (1998), who attempts to tease out the philosophical and practical distinctions which individuals face in their everyday social worlds. Harré points out that knowing is a complex relational concept. He differentiates between the 'knower and the known' and argues that unlike the natural sciences, in the social sciences, the 'knower is part of the known.' This certainly seems to be the case for these education students. The students entering this particular programme were not constructing themselves as 'knowers', at least in terms of the specialised language being used in their initial studies. Although many of these students would be seen as knowers to their own students and would be specialised in their own body of knowledge, their status as knower was being challenged and called into question by the new context, and by their conceptualisation of themselves as students.

Part of the students' challenge in this study was, as Harré argues, making sense of the social world (in this case within education), which can often create ontological illusions which blur our senses in trying to map out and understand that world. To understand any aspect of the social world, he argues, we need only to grasp the local grammar. Harré's analysis offers us a means of thinking what it is students encounter when they enter an (un)known entity, the university, which is also imbued with status and power. Harré's deconstruction process offers a means of questioning the language, the practices and the procedures that occur within a particular aspect of the social world, as ways of 'knowing' that are coded within varying discourses. This last point is illustrated by Craig's difficulty with the language being used by the tutors on his course:

> Craig: 'Fighting your way through educational jargon especially for me who's been a working person with no educational background it was difficult.'

Students themselves were offering up rationales as to why, individually, they thought they were finding it so difficult and some were clearly taking solace from their peers who were also finding parts of the course difficult. What was apparent was that a large number of interviewees were internalising their difficulties and seeing these as 'shortcomings' within themselves; many were questioning their ability to complete the course or whether they were 'teacher material,' which could be translated as 'I can't be that sort of 'knower.'" This seemed to be a particular discourse in which individual anxiety was being channelled into the notion that they were possibly not capable of taking this next step on the education pathway. For example:

> Alex: 'Also you think is this the right thing for me to do can I do this am I not kidding myself that maybe I can't do this year maybe last year but perhaps I can't perhaps it's beyond my abilities?'

> Susie: 'There is all these nagging doubts you know, God am I teacher material you know?'

There was ample evidence that students were not seeing the structural factors affecting their transition but were using their difficulties as evidence of their own perceived lack of ability to study at this level, which was clearly increasing their anxiety still further:

> Sarah: 'Am I clever enough to do this? Dents the confidence a little bit when others have very clever things to say'

> Anna: 'Although I know I can teach and I think I know I can do it well perhaps I'm not an academic perhaps that second year is too much.'

Language was heavily imbued with a whole set of pre-suppositions and characteristics. This was particularly the case around the word 'academic' which inheres in the entire discourse of HE. This word, which came up repeatedly was emotionally loaded and needed individual definition, as students appeared to be constructing it in different ways. There seemed to be many barriers associated with defining, owning, and applying this word, particularly to themselves; often it was used as a means of demarcating themselves from others. No respondent self-identified as an academic but many of the respondents dis-identified and said they were *not* academic.

> Tim: 'I just think it's going back to my point about being academic, being technical and the language. I just feel if we hadn't had all the academic language to start with and they had used normal English, normal language... I mean how many people talk about being didactic and discourse, I mean why can't you just say a conversation?'

This particular aspect of the data exposed a powerful discourse in which the structures of education and what was seen as being an academic appeared to be regulating, and in some cases preventing, students moving forward, as well as initiating a sense of 'otherness.' The following students had sub-divided the group and positioned themselves accordingly:

> Tim: 'It's like you've got the artys against the academics...there is a pocket of people who are academically bright or academically *au fait* with what's going on. But there's another group of people who are the non-academic types or who have not been in education for a while who are finding it difficult.'

Not only did the word 'academia' conjure up images about what was expected in terms of the educational process but the institution, the university, was also being constructed within a particular context. This was especially pertinent with students who had come via the Further Education route, where university was seen as a step up in terms of educational achievement and expectations. Millie used a school analogy to describe how she viewed her transition on to this course:

> Millie: 'I've gone a little bit up-market I think...it's like starting off in the reception class and school and then you work your way up and you get more serious as you go.'
>
> Max: 'I'm now at university, I'm grown up.'
>
> Emily: 'This feels really grown-up and academic.'
>
> Martha: 'We're from a practical field and we are not high achievers. Others on the course seem to have got it sussed there are better people in the group they're on the ball they've got the jargon off I feel like I want to stay within what I know.'

When it was suggested to them that they might be seen as high achievers by their students, one of the group was very well-qualified and from a semi-professional background, one replied with:

> Martha: 'We're teachers and they're lecturers.'

These students had constructed 'lecturer' as something above and beyond the role of a 'teacher'. On further probing the university lecturer was seen as higher; if we think of Harré's distinction it could again be argued that they were saying 'I'm not that sort of knower':

Martha: 'They have a degree and a higher level of education and certain specialisms they show us what's expected.'

This interviewee with her own subject specialism and other educational qualifications seemed unable to accept that she was probably no different from the lecturers who taught her. There was a reluctance for two of the group members to accept this rationale and it brought us back again to the role of language whereby particular words, such as 'academic', or 'lecturer', were imbued with a myriad of meanings. Earlier messages, combined with the students' social and educational background, mediated through their *habitus*, resulted in how they defined or aligned with particular words.

It could be argued that what Martha and her peers were experiencing was what Bourdieu would suggest is the class distribution of educational opportunities: people live within a framework of opportunities and constraints that structure their life chances. This structuring is internalised and ultimately, as it is lived, 'naturally' shapes the world individuals live within, (Nash, 1990). In other words, individuals start to act as if it were true. Therefore, from this research, it would seem that the WP agenda must fully identify the tangible and the non-tangible 'barriers' that prevent students from being 'at ease' in their educational surroundings, much of which is played out amongst an outmoded backdrop of not being 'good enough' or 'clever enough' to be studying at HE level. Thus far, there is a paucity of research to help us identify this aspect of the students' transition and progression within the HE sector.

A further dimension of the discourses within the group was that of those who would have been considered 'academic' by their peers, far from forging ahead, had started to modify their behaviour in order to meet with approval in their peer group. These students may well have seen themselves as 'knowers' yet they were actively distancing themselves from being positioned as 'knowers' by others in the group. The group itself appeared to be operating a regulating mechanism by which others were both surveilling and moderating their behaviour accordingly, as both Jack and Richard demonstrate:

Jack: 'I realise that others are struggling but I hold back a bit because I don't want to be seen as a know-all. Also I don't want to set myself up within the group whereby I'm seen as the one oh yeah Jack knows how to do that he'll do that.'

Richard: 'I felt as if I was being a bit staid sticking to one style of learning I always want to undertake a full rigorous analysis of whatever I am dealing with. I felt I was being labelled [by the group] it was as if it was just go with the flow we don't want to do this anyway.'

Resistance

Pockets of resistance to the dominant discourses were occurring, some overtly and others more subtly. Whilst students may have been caught up within the educational socialisation process, clearly they were resisting and employing strategies to regain some of their own sense of power. For example, Adrian comments that his group does not allow tutors to carry on in accordance with their lesson plan if they, the students, do not understand what is being said:

Adrian: 'We just don't allow them to get away with it...a hand goes up and it's 'don't understand that please explain' and the tutor has to stop and go over it.'

Another group decided that they were going to organise themselves into groups before they were asked to and almost 'band together' in a kind of 'them and us' situation:

Tim: '...in fact they [tutors] got very angry that the sort of arty lot had gone off and grouped together. We'd automatically decided this is how we are going to work and I think they resented that.'

Further evidence of resistance came from Tim and Hannah when they were discussing people who use language as a means to make themselves look more intellectual [both tutors and students]. When asked how the group managed that they replied:

Hannah: 'It does happen quite subtly and people say 'oh yes' to pretend that they know what they mean I know I have or I just sit there and don't say anything sometimes I just can't be bothered to stop things.'

Tim also started to question the motives for his learning; whilst this may not be seen as resistance *per se*, Tim was resisting the discourse of seeing both the lecturer and the education process as something so powerful that it cannot be challenged:

Tim: 'Am I learning or am I writing this to please you to get through an exam or am I writing it to say that it makes sense to me so that I will be a good teacher? I'm writing this to get the flipping bit of paper at the end of the day which doesn't mean to say that it has any relevance to how I personally feel or bear any relevance on how I'm going to teach and I find that quite hypocritical as well.'

Some students just wanted to get it 'right' before saying anything to ensure they didn't look foolish. As Kuhn (1995) states, one of the central politics of class is the feeling of 'not getting it right'. Equally, Bourdieu (1974) would argue that through the habitus the 'elite' class, meaning those who are assured and familiar within educational structures, will demoralise students from lower social class groups through their self-assuredness, confidence and the ease with which they interact within the education system :

> Ellie: 'I want to know that I'm correct before I say anything...I would feel silly...' [if I asked a stupid question].

> Kerrie: 'We do have a good discussion about it generally but the thing generally in human nature being when you are amongst people if you don't know you don't want to look an idiot.'

On probing Caitlin as to why she was not asking for clarification from the tutor she replied:

> 'When Jeff (tutor) is talking like this it's all very challenging and I can't really talk about it because I don't know what I'm talking about yet I'm still trying to get it right up here.'

We can see from the students' reticence to speak out, in an environment which is designed for them to question and explore, that Earwaker (1992) is right to argue that entry into Higher Education is like any other unfamiliar game, where the rules have to be learned and the skills practised to be able to join in fully.

Concluding comments

In this chapter we have highlighted the discourses, power relations and resistances that were occurring for one group of students on a Cert. Ed/PGCE programme, many of whom were non-traditional entrants, and on the course, to some extent, as the result of WP. Having data from a full academic year would have been useful to perhaps be able to identify at which point students were able to move beyond their resistances and what factors enabled them to do that. The issue of WP is a 'hot' political topic. Recently in the *Guardian* education supplement, Ted Wragg correctly points out that it is right for the government to continue with WP initiatives but that if universities gamble on less qualified entrants, they must be supported and not vilified if some students drop out. Importantly, Wragg points out that 'vulnerable students teeter on the brink and need massive support.' This last point, sadly, is not often reflected in student support mechanisms or in staffing levels. By all means give individuals the opportunity to study within HE, but support them in that journey, do not offer them 'old wine in new bottles.' By this we mean offering students the promise of an environment of 'inclusion' and of truly widening participation, when what they are actually given is a system littered with barriers and not much different from what they have experienced first time around, when school was seen as part of the process of marginalisation, rather than as part of the answer to their problems, (MacFadden, 1995).

O'Toole (2002) questions whether policy commitments to Widening Participation are reality or empty rhetoric (cited in Reay *et al.*, 2002a). True evaluation of the success or otherwise of WP must ensure that the high emotional and personal costs mature students face is part of that process. In terms of their fear and anxiety when faced with the psycho-social structural factors associated with the education process, many students mediate through a notion of *habitus* that is central to the WP debate; in policy discourses this is still overlooked.

Notes

1   Entry level teaching qualification which, as well as being a 'stand alone' teaching qualification, acts as approved prior learning for year one of the two- year part time Cert. Ed. programme.
2   National Vocational Qualifications
3   General Certificates of Education and Advanced level General Certificates of Education
4   Certainly in Group 1 interviews we did not ascertain S/E background, but indicators of social class were given by the interviewees narratives, however, we need to proceed with caution before making any claims about social class, access and transition to HE.

Bibliography

Archer, L, Hutchings, M and Ross, A (2003) *Higher Education and Social Class: Issues of exclusion and inclusion.* London: Routledge Falmer

Bourdieu, P (1977) *Outline of a Theory of Practice.* Cambridge: CUP

Connor, H et al (1999) *Making the right choice: how students choose universities and colleges.* London: Institute of Employment Studies/Committee of Vice Chancellors and Principals

Daloz, L A (1990) *Effective Teaching and Mentoring*. Oxford: Jossey-Bass Publishers

Davies, P and Williams, J (2001) For me or Not for Me? Fragility and Risk in Mature Students' Decision-making, in *Higher Education Quarterly*, 55(2): April 185-203

Department for Education and Skills (DfES) (2003) *The Future of Higher Education*. London: HMSO

Earwaker, J (1992) *Helping and Supporting Students*. The Society for the Research into Higher Education: Buckingham Open University

Green, P and Webb, S (1997) Student voices: Alternative Routes, Alternative Identities, in: Williams, J (ed) *Negotiating Access to Higher Education: The discourse of selectivity and equity*. Buckingham: Open University

Harré, R (1998) When the Knower is also the Known, in: May, T, and Williams, M (eds) *Knowing the Social World*. Buckingham: Open University

Jenkins, R (1992) *Pierre Bourdieu*. London: Routledge

Kuhn, A (1995) *Family Secrets: Acts of Memory and Imagination*. London: Verso

MacFadden, M. (1995) 'Second Chance' Education?: Settling old scores, in: *Journal of Access Studies*, 10(1): 40-59

Mann, S (2001) Alternative Perspectives on the Student Experience: Alienation and Engagement, in: *Studies in Higher Education*, 26(1): 7-19

Nash, R (1990) Bourdieu on Education and Social and Cultural Reproduction, in: *British Journal of Sociology of Education*, 11(4): 431-447

O'Toole, G (2000) Included or Excluded? Mature Students in HE. Paper presented at the British Educational Research Association Conference University of Cardiff 7-9 September

Reay, D, Ball, S and David, M (2002a) It's taking me a long time but I'll get there in the end: mature students on access courses and higher education choice, in: *British Educational Research Journal*, 28(1): 5-19

Reay, D, Davies, J, David, M and Ball, S (2001) Choices of degree or degrees of choice? Class, 'Race' and the Higher Education Choice Process, in: *Sociology*, 35(4): 855-874

Reay, D (2002b) Class, authenticity and the transition to higher education for mature students, in: *Sociological Review*, 50(3): August 398-419

Satterthwaite, J (2003) The Terror! The Terror! Speaking the Literal to Inspire the Understanding of a Friend, in: Satterthwaite, J, Atkinson, E and Gale, K. *Discourse, Power and Resistance: Challenging the Rhetoric of Contemporary Education*. Staffordshire: Trentham Books

Swartz, D (1997) *Culture and Power: The work of Pierre Bourdieu*. London: University of Chicago Press

Warrington, P (2003) Aspirations of Access for HE Students, in: *British Journal of Sociology of Education*, 24(1): 95-108

Weil, S (1989) Access: towards education or miseducation? Adults imagine the future, in: Fulton, O (ed). *Access and Institutional Change*. Milton Keynes: Society for Research into Higher Education/Open University Press

Woodley, A and Wilson, J (2002) British Higher Education and its Older Clients, in Higher Education, 44: 329-347

Wragg, T (2003) Give Hodge a Holiday. http://education.guardian.co.uk/higher/comment/story

11

Telling stories about learners and learning

ROGER HARRISON

Roger Harrison analyses the effect of using metaphors of the journey in educational discourse, examining in particular the ways in which these metaphors legitimate certain ways of understanding education and silence others. He shows that metaphor is never neutral: that the construction through metaphor of the learner as traveller constrains the practice of student and tutor alike, constructing learning as linear and progressive: straight and narrow. We need, he argues, a more generous narrative of learning. It is not only participation that should be widened: learning itself needs to be more inclusively imagined. Harrison's argument leads directly to the further analysis offered by Tamsin Haggis in the concluding chapter.

Introduction

'What is truth but a mobile army of metaphors.' (Nietsche)

I want to frame this analysis within an idea of narrative, with its suggestion that it is the story telling capacity of human beings which is central to their nature (MacIntyre, 1981). It is through telling stories that we both come to understand the world and attempt to impose our own understandings on the world. As Edwards and Usher put this:

> The social world is made 'present', storied or narrated into being through the discursive practices in which we engage and which make our experiences meaningful. (Edwards and Usher, 1996:217)

The word 'narrative' has its roots in Latin words for both 'knowing' (*gnarus*) and 'telling' (*narro*)). These two sides of its etymology are significant in revealing the work which narrative performs. It is a tool for knowing as well as telling, for absorbing knowledge as well as expressing it (Porter Abbott, 2002). It shows knowledge as fluid and in transition, since meaning is always altered in the narration depending on who is talking, who is listening and the conditions which pertain at the time. In the context of our own professional field, each of us tells our own story, rooted in a unique autobiographical trajectory, but at the same time embedded in the history and traditions of our disciplinary fields, which are in turn grounded in the wider narratives of our culture. Following the idea that truths are constructed through narratives allows us to ask questions about how certain narratives get constructed, what sort of materials are used and what effects they produce. As Jonathan Potter puts this:

> Reality enters into human practices by way of the categories and descriptions that are part of those practices. The world is not ready categorised by God or nature in ways that we are all forced to accept. It is constituted in one way or another as people talk it, write it and argue it. (Potter, 1996: 98)

Attention is given not only to categories, descriptions and the ways in which they construct certain objects as knowable and known, but also the techniques through which certain descriptions are worked up to become more persuasive than others, effectively marginalising or silencing alternative accounts. These processes of production are not neutral or naturally occurring. Rather they are political, contestable and open to critical analysis.

The particular narrative I want to focus on in this chapter is that which draws on the metaphor of learning as a journey and learners as travellers. This arose from attendance at a conference at the end of 2002 organised by the Learning and Skills Development Agency in the UK. The conference was titled 'Learners' Journeys'. This metaphor not only provided the title for the conference but also for a Learning and Skills Development Agency (LSDA) funded research project and the theme of the autumn 2002 edition of the LSDA's journal. The LSDA clearly thought there was mileage in the idea. They were by no means alone in conceiving learning in terms of 'routes', 'pathways' or 'journeys', and learners as individual travellers who are continually making choices about pace, direction and destination. It prompted me to explore further the metaphor of learning as a journey; to examine those understandings and attendant possibilities which it suggests, and those which it silences. The aim is to examine in more detail the origins and implications of this metaphor in constructing stories about learning and the learner. The chapter is in three parts. First, a review of the role of metaphors as carriers of meaning and of the philosophical assumptions about language which underpin our understandings of the nature of this role. Second, an exploration of some of the assumptions, beliefs and tacit understandings which are suggested by dominant metaphors of learning. Third, an indication of some alternative metaphors of learning which bring into play theories of learning which are marginalised or silenced by the journey metaphor, and which serve to open up spaces in which we might think differently about learning and learners.

Metaphor and meaning

A significant literature has grown up around the use of metaphor as a means of understanding and explaining the world around us. A key distinction which runs through this literature is between understandings of language as a neutral and transparent medium through which reality can be precisely described, which is the position of, logical positivism, and the view that how we come to understand the world is through a process of mental 'construction' (Ortony,1979). According to the logical positivist or 'purist' perspective, metaphor is simply a block to the clear and transparent communication of meaning between language users. Within the positivist tradition metaphor is viewed as an ornamental or ambiguous use of language, quite unsuited to scientific or philosophical discourse.

In contrast, the constructionist perspective views metaphors as significant, not as a source of literal descriptions of reality, but as a means of making sense of our concrete experience of the world and of explaining abstract concepts and theories. Rather than merely a rhetorical flourish, Lakoff and Johnson suggest that metaphor is fundamental to our processes of meaning making:

> ...metaphor is pervasive in everyday life, not just in language, but in thought and action. Our ordinary conceptual system, in terms of which we both think and act, is fundamentally metaphorical in nature. (Lakoff and Johnson, 1980, p3)

From this perspective our understandings are the outcome of a complex interaction between the information given, the context in which this takes place and the knower's pre-existing knowledge. This allows for a more dynamic concept of language, one which acknowledges the role of context, culture and history in the giving and taking of meanings. Language consistently refuses to comply with the 'essentialist' requirement that words carry the same meaning for all people in all places at all times. The making of meanings becomes an artful linguistic game in which we all participate through the activities of speaking, writing or signing.

> Knowing how to use a word, like knowing how to cast a fly, is not knowing about some special kind of object. Like knowing how to play tennis or swim, it is a skill. (Aspin, quoted in Taylor, 1984:26)

It is the generative nature of metaphors, the ways in which they engage us in the linguistic game playing through which meaning is made and through which it can be challenged, that is the subject of this chapter.

Metaphors gain much of their power and persuasiveness though association with other metaphors, forming entire networks of understanding which might grow out of a single 'root metaphor'. Lakoff and Johnson (1980) give the example of 'argument' understood through the metaphor of 'war'. Putting this in the context of academic writing, when you finish reading this chapter you might want to 'attack my position', suggest that my claims are 'indefensible', and so 'demolish' my arguments. I might even be 'shot down in flames'. Part of the conceptual network associated with war is being used here to partially characterise the concept of academic debate, and in the process to show that how we understand, talk about, and perform debates might be structured by that association. Evidence for the power of metaphor in shaping and structuring how we think and act is provided by the difficulty of imagining a world in which argument is viewed differently, for example as a dance in which the main objective is to achieve an elegant and balanced performance. Substituting the metaphor of the dance for that of war would entirely change how we experience, enact and talk about argument (Lakoff and Johnson, 1980).

Metaphors can carry with them not only a set of understandings about how things are but also the suggestion of how things might change. In the context of social policy planning Donald Schön (1979) has examined the stories people tell in characterising problems through metaphors which subtly and insidiously suggest certain solutions. Thus if slums are described in terms of a cancer they are recognised as something which is bad, and must be isolated and treated. In this sense metaphors are generative; they contain meanings and associations which constrain and sometimes control those actions and strategies which are seen as possible or desirable. Schön argues that in order to think differently about entrenched problems in the field of urban planning it is first necessary to restructure the frame within which these problems are understood. In this sense, this chapter is attempting to take a tentative step towards frame restructuring in relation to understandings of learning.

Stories about learners and journeys

Turning now to the 'Learners' Journeys' conference itself, the associations or networks of meaning suggested by the organisers were further elucidated in the conference details. Here we learn that 'personal choices' and 'individual aspiration' are vital to the workings of the education and training system and that the challenge facing educators is to 'create coherent and rewarding pathways that satisfy all types of potential learners'. The literature of and about lifelong learning is imbued with the language of goals and outcomes, routes and pathways, maps and mazes, barriers and bridges, stages and progression. The root metaphor here might be characterised as the purposeful life, emerging from the Judaeo-Christian tradition aptly represented in John Bunyan's *The Pilgrim's Progress*. Contemporary ideas about learning can be traced back to this tradition in that learning is assumed to be purposeful and progressive, and individuals are expected to act autonomously in planning their pursuit of previously identified goals. As Bunyan's pilgrim discovers, the route is sometimes complicated and confusing, with many alternative pathways and little effective signposting, requiring inputs of advice and guidance from those more familiar with the terrain and the rules of conduct.

The OECD report *Pathways for Learning* (1989) represents this understanding in the context of post-compulsory education as 'a stage of transition' between school and Higher Education, or between school and work, with the attendant issues of clear progression routes and guidance:

> ...the concept of transition... does point up the need for adequate guidance and counselling, and for flexibility in the access to and sequence of courses in order to accommodate changes of direction in students' educational paths. (OECD, 1989: 11)

The CBI report 'Routes for Success' (1993) links the idea of learning as a journey with the notion of 'careership', in which individuals navigate their own career progression with the assistance of a 'Careership profile', revitalised careers guidance and reformed frameworks of vocational credit. The durability of the journey metaphor and the role this ascribes to both learners and the guidance services is illustrated by this extract from a report on a DfEE funded project in the mid-1990s :

> The complexity of the journey, the experience and the skill of the traveller and the quality of the guidance will all affect the extent to which the journey is undertaken without anxiety. (Della Fazey, 1996: 30)

The metaphor of journey has exercised, and still does exercise, a powerful influence on how we understand the nature of learning and the roles of teachers and learners. It provides a discursive context in which related ideas such as 'ladders of learning', 'routes for success' or 'pathways to opportunity' are easily assimilated, and in which policy developments such as credit accumulation and transfer, targets and learning outcomes are readily understood. Each refers to the progressive and cumulative nature of the journey, in which arrival at certain pre-determined staging posts is recognised through qualifications or portfolio entries.

It is a view of learning which fits well with current policy imperatives, in particular the requirement to identify, measure and assess all forms of learning at the level of individual achievement. It forms part of the economic rationale for investing public money in lifelong learning, based on the logic that it will eventually yield results in terms of economic productivity and global competitive advantage. To sustain this claim requires hard evidence of individual learning outcomes, which has in turn led to the development of a complex machinery of specification and measurement, locking practitioners into technical and rational frameworks and procedures. As Eraut *et al* (2000) express it, the dominant paradigm in education and training 'treats learning as a self-conscious, deliberate, goal driven process which is planned and organised by 'providers' to yield outcomes that are easily described and measured' (232). Whilst arguably effective in relation to at least some aspects of formal learning, it is a paradigm which fails to capture the richness and complexity of learning, as Eraut and colleagues describe in their detailed study of learning in the workplace.

The image of the learner on a journey also carries over into research, with implications for the ways in which we frame our research questions and the methodologies we employ in attempting to answer them. The LSDA research report referred to earlier (LSDA, 2002) describes an imaginative approach to research in which informants are encouraged to use the learning journey metaphor to help them describe their own learning experiences. For example, a respondent who was frustrated by his slow progress was able to say:

> Well, I'm just on the motorway. There's a lot of cars holding me up and I want to get to London quick. (LSDA, 2002: 29)

The stories elicited through this methodology clearly have value and provide real insights into the lived experience of these learners, but what is not acknowledged is the power of metaphor in allowing the emergence of some accounts whilst silencing others. If we understand metaphor not as a neutral descriptor of how things are but as an active player in the construction of meaning, then interviewees are already both enabled and constrained in the sorts of stories they can tell. What we are hearing is not, the clear and transparent voices of learners telling their own stories, but learners working within predetermined discursive parameters. Metaphors of journeys, roads, bridges and junctions are effective in mobilising certain understandings of the learning process and enabling learners to articulate certain aspects of their learning experience, but at the same time they place limits on what can be said, thought or written. What is being indicated here is the effect of metaphor in opening up certain spaces for thinking and talking about learning, whilst simultaneously closing down others. Roads and bridges can only take you so far.

The 'learner's journeys' metaphor not only shapes our understandings of learners' experiences, it also shapes our understandings of the outcomes of learning. The language of goals and outcomes suggests learning as an individual possession, something which can be acquired.

> This approach... brings to mind the activity of accumulating material goods. The language of 'knowledge acquisition' and 'concept development' makes us think about the human mind as a container to be filled with certain materials and about the learner as becoming the owner of these materials. (Sfard, 1998, 5)

Knowledge becomes the baggage we carry with us on the journey; a material and stable commodity; something which can be moved about between the mind of a teacher and that of a learner, or between one practice setting and another, without changing its nature or meaning. The quantity and nature of the knowledge we carry with us can be assessed at any point, in the way that baggage is checked and weighed at an airport. The notion of learning as 'acquisition' suggests a positivist view of knowledge and a transmission model of learning, in which the learner's role is to annex the knowledge of others and the role of the teacher is to assemble it into manageable chunks which can be more easily added to the learner's existing collection. Reflective learning, whilst in some ways representing a radical break from the transmission model, is still understood as a cognitive process, something which occurs in the mind of the learner, and knowledge remains an individual possession. The image of knowledge as an entity which exists outside ourselves, floating free of context, is deeply embedded in much of the literature about learning and finds expression in our habitual ways of speaking and thinking.

In addition, the metaphor of the learner as traveller suggests a certain category of person: an autonomous and enterprising individual, rationally choosing the mode, pace, direction and destination of his or her journey. At its most persuasive the image of learners we are presented with is that of freewheeling individuals, actively constructing meanings for themselves, adding to their existing store of knowledge, using their own judgement and feelings as they evaluate and select learning opportunities. In this sense learners are seen as having seized the controls and taken on the self-steering capacities of the independent and autonomous individual. The theory of learning which fits most comfortably with this image is reflection (Kolb, 1984; Brook-field, 1987; Boud and Walker, 1998). It is through reflection, these authors claim, that learners are able to make informed decisions and choices, taking into account not only the complexities of the context or the problem, but also their own tacit knowledge, assumptions and values. One effect of this pervasive idea has been a proliferation of curriculum innovations designed to foster processes of reflection, planning and decision making, resulting in a rash of profiles, port-folios, records of achievement and learning logs in all sectors of post-compulsory education (Harrison, 2000). The primacy of reflection as the dominant model for learning also extends to professional develop-ment (Schön, 1983), with significant implication for how our own professional performance is assessed. Here, educational discourses and practices can be understood as actively involved in the shaping of subjectivities, cultivating the self-steering capacities of the individual, making possible certain forms of engagement with learning and teach-ing at the same time as excluding others.

Whilst theories of reflective learning appear to offer learners the keys to the highway, sociological, philosophical and cultural critiques point to the ways in which the terrain itself, and the routes through that terrain, are already circumscribed and constrained, offering little space for the exercise of individual autonomy. Institutional structures, funding régimes and qualification systems all work to ensure that some learning journeys are less stressful than others. Pedagogic, pas-toral and financial support is provided for learners aiming for those outcomes which contribute towards national and local targets for learning, usually expressed in terms of qualifications or employment outcomes. Cutting across country can be difficult and laborious work, whilst staying on well-trodden pathways is usually easier on the pocket as well as the footwear.

An emphasis on the qualities and characteristics of individual travel-lers has tended to shift attention away from the characteristics of the terrain and the conditions in which travel is undertaken. Techniques of reflection and action planning are most effective when the informa-tion available is complete, and future trends are predictable. In the context of a globalised economy and a risk society, neither of these conditions can be met, leaving individual choice as a risky rather than a rational business (Beck, 1994). Being lost at sea without a compass may be a more appropriate metaphor for the contemporary learner than that of the purposeful and goal oriented traveller. Following this line of critique we might view as significant the emergence of metaphors of learning journeys, with all their attendant baggage of meanings, at precisely the time when social and economic conditions make their realisation uniquely problematic.

Re-telling the story

The argument of this chapter has been that metaphors are both powerful in their effects and extensive in their reach. It follows that by changing the metaphor we would expect to see profound changes in how we understand processes of teaching, learning and assessment, and that these in turn would have fundamental implications for the way we organise learning and support learners. If, for example, we were to view learning as a product of participation in social practices (Lave and Wenger, 1991), rather than an individual achievement; as something which occurs in the 'in between space' between teacher and learner (Vanderstraeten and Biesta, 2001: 7) rather than in the mind of any one individual; or as 'co-emergence, at the intersection of invention, identity and environment' (Fenwick, 2001: 243), rather than as a steady progression towards pre-planned goals, then the priorities of policy and the focus for research might look very different. Within these more social understandings of learning the heroic individual learner is relegated from the centre of the stage to a subsidiary role as participant in a collective process of negotiating meaning within a particular context and community of practice. By suggesting that learning can *only* be understood as a social process, traditional preoccupations with what goes on in the mind of the individual are displaced. Here it is not the learner but the whole social and cultural context in which learning takes place which occupies the centre of the theoretical frame. The idea of knowledge as a stable commodity that belongs to an individual and can be transmitted, assessed and accredited is undermined by this narrative of learning, with significant implications for supporting and accrediting learners.

A substantial body of research literature is already available to those who might want to travel 'off road', shifting the focus of attention from the linear progression of learning to 'the complex, organic character of the learning engagement' (Davis and Sumara, 2000:

842). Further exploration of these alternative theories and the metaphorical possibilities they suggest is beyond the scope of this chapter. However, the point is made that the meanings we ascribe to learning, and the identity categories in which we place learners, are not self evident or given. Rather they are constructed through language and are open to challenge and change. Learners, and those whose professional role is to support learners, are not only narrated into being by the stories of learning, they are also the narrators of these stories. Authority in this context 'is never a fixed or closed régime', but rather 'an endless and open strategic game' (Gordon, 1991: 5). The stories we tell are neither stable or universal, but constantly in play and always containing the seeds of their own contradictions, as well as the possibilities for 'thinking differently', for envisaging new ways of understanding learning and learners.

I would like to end with a quote from Davis and Sumara (2000) who have drawn on images and metaphors from biology and ecology as a means of understanding processes of knowledge formation:

> ...people are not fumbling along a more-or-less straight road towards a totalizing and self-contained knowledge of the universe. Rather, they are all taking part in structuring knowledge... and this requires a completely different image. (Davis and Sumara, 2000: 821)

Such an image, or images, offer at least the possibility for thinking differently about the processes of learning, teaching and assessment, and could provide the discursive resources with which to tell alternative stories about learners and the processes of knowledge construction.

References

Aspin, D (1984) Metaphor and Meaning in Educational Discourse, in: Taylor, W (ed) *Metaphors of Education*. London: Heinman

Beck, U (1994) The Reinvention of Politics: Towards a Theory of Reflexive Modernisation, in: Beck, U Giddens, A and Lash, S. *Reflexive Modernisation: Politics, Tradition and Aesthetics in Modern Social Order*. Cambridge: Polity Press

Boud, D and Walker, D (1998) Promoting reflection in professional courses: the challenge of context, in: *Studies in Higher Education*, Vol 23 (2), 191-206

Brookfield, S (1987) Developing Critical Thinkers: challenging adults to explore alternative ways of thinking and acting. Milton Keynes: Open University

Coffield, F (2000) Introduction: A critical analysis of the concept of a learning society, in: Coffield, F (ed) *Differing visions of a Learning Society, Volume 1.* Bristol: The Policy Press.

Confederation of British Industry (1993) *Routes for Success.* London: CBI.

Davis, B and Sumara, D (2000) Curriculum forms: on the assumed shapes of knowing and knowledge, in: *Journal of Curriculum Studies*, Vol 32, No 6, 821-845

Edwards, R and Usher, R (1996) What Stories Do I Tell Now? New times and new narratives for the adult educator, in: *International Journal of Lifelong Education,* Vol. 13, No. 3, 216-229

Eraut, M, Alderton, J, Cole, G and Senker, P (2000) Development of knowledge and skills at work, in: Coffield, F (ed) *Differing visions of a Learning Society,* Vol 1. Bristol: The Policy Press

Fazey, D (1996) Guidance for Learner Autonomy, in: McNair, S. *Putting Learners at the Centre: Reflections from the Guidance and Learner Autonomy in Higher Education Programme.* Sheffield: DfEE

Fenwick, T (2001) Work knowing 'on the fly': enterprise cultures and co-emergent epistemologies, in: *Studies in Continuing Education*, Vol 23, No 2: 243-259

Gordon, C (1991) Introduction, in Graham, G, Gordon, C and Miller, P. *The Foucault Effect: studies in governmentality.* London: Harvester Wheatsheaf.

Harrison, R (2000) Learner managed learning: managing to learn or learning to manage? in: *International Journal of Lifelong Education*, Vol 19, No 4, 312-321

Kolb, D (1984) *Experiential Learning.* New Jersey: Prentice Hall

Lakoff, G and Johnson, M (1980) *Metaphors we live by.* Chicago: University of Chicago Press

Lave, J and Wenger, E (1991) *Situated Learning: legitimate peripheral participation.* Cambridge: Cambridge University Press

MacIntyre, A (1981) *After Virtue.* London: Duckworth

Organisation for Economic Co-operation and Development (1989) *Pathways for Learning: Education and Training from 16-19.* Paris: OECD

Orteny, A (1979) Metaphor: A Multidimensional Problem, in: Orteny, A (ed) *Metaphor and Thought.* Cambridge: Cambridge University Press

Porter Abbott, H (2002) *The Cambridge Introduction to Narrative.* Cambridge: Cambridge University Press

Potter, J (1996) *Representing Reality: discourse, rhetoric and social construction.* London: Sage.

Schön, D (1979) Generative Metaphor: A Perspective on Problem Setting in Social Policy, in: Orteny, A (ed) *Metaphor and Thought.* Cambridge: Cambridge University Press

Schön, D (1983) *The reflective practitioner.* London: Temple Smith

Sfard, A 1998) On two metaphors of learning and the dangers of choosing just one, in: *Educational Researcher,* Vol 27, No 2: 4-13

Vanderstraeten, R and Biesta, G (2001) How is education possible? Preliminary investigations for a theory of education, in: *Educational Philosophy and Theory,* Vol 33, No1: 7-21.

12

Constructions of learning in higher education: metaphor, epistemology, and complexity

TAMSIN HAGGIS

Tamsin Haggis continues and extends the analysis of the previous chapter, looking at the images chosen by students themselves as they come to terms with, and find metaphors for, their experience of learning. This chapter exposes the differences and similarities between learner discourses and official discourses of Higher Education learning theory, suggesting that the meaning of learning is articulated for students by their choices of imagery, choices from which teachers should learn.

Despite the voluminous literature on teaching and learning across the different sectors and domains, there is a marked tendency to simplify learning rather than deal with its complexity. Richard Pring (2000) has commented on the tendency in educational research to ignore the complexity of learning. Future educational research, he asserts, must attend to what it means to learn and that requires a careful analysis of many different sorts of learning. Cullen *et al*, 2002:115 (Tavistock Report)

Although the complex nature of learning is discussed in some recent studies (see Savin-Baden, 2000; Light and Cox, 2001), the literatures of mainstream Higher Education pedagogical theory (eg. Prosser *et. al.*, 2003; Biggs, 1999), and related policy documents which make use of such theory (eg. HEFC, 1999; 2001), continue to work largely with the established model of learning associated with the idea of deep and surface approaches to a university learning task[1]. This model has expanded over the years to include a wide variety of different research interpretations, and also, in some cases, an increasing variety of elements (eg. Entwistle, 2000). Despite this attempt to address the complexity of factors involved, however, the overall conceptual framework remains largely unchanged, arguably reflecting a fairly one-dimensional, institutional perspective, which reflects institutional agendas (Haggis, 2003). As policy initiatives bring increasing numbers of non-traditional students into a changing Higher Education sector, the certainties underpinning this view of learning are being challenged, arguably suggesting the need to look again at what is understood by learning (and, indeed, non-learning) in this context.

This chapter sets out to explore the ways in which learning in Higher Education is discussed by a group of learners, as opposed to how it is discussed by theorists and policy makers[2]. This will be done through examining metaphors in the talk of a group of mature students who are about to embark upon a university access course. Questions will then be raised about the type of analysis which underpins this discussion, and an alternative analysis will be explored which will attempt to look at description and metaphor from a different epistemological perspective, that of complexity and non-linear/dynamic systems theory (Cilliers, 1998; Bosma and Kunnen, 2001).

The analysis forms part of a longitudinal study which aims to explore individual narratives about learning in Higher Education, first on an Access[3] course, and then at undergraduate level. Its focus, overall, is the processes involved in study (reading, writing essays etc.), analysed in conjunction with the participants' stories about school, family, employment and post-school learning history. Narratives about these processes are considered in the context of ideas expressed about learning, talk about the nature and purposes of Higher Education, and in the context of work and life beyond the university.

This chapter reports on one aspect of an analysis of the first round of interviews, which were conducted before the participants had begun their Access course. A new cohort of university Access students in Scotland were invited to take part in the research project by letter, which was sent out after they had been accepted onto the Access course, and before they had begun the first block. Twelve participants (six women and six men, aged from 26 to over 60) came for an initial group meeting to discuss the purpose, nature, and limits of the project. The participants were later interviewed individually. These interviews aimed to explore the various contexts surrounding the participants' decision to enter university, and focused on questions around topics such as family background, educational experience, qualifications, employment history, and talk around concepts such as 'learning', 'student', 'teacher' and 'essay'. All the topic areas were covered in each interview, but the order and direction of the questions was determined by the responses of each individual (for further discussion of the methodology and analysis see Haggis, forthcoming)

Metaphors of learning: a standard data analysis

Research in the area of metaphor suggests that, far from being mere figures of speech, metaphors 'constitute an essential mechanism of the mind' (Martinez *et. al.*, 2001:965). The creation and use of metaphor, it is argued, helps people to 'see what is invisible, to describe what otherwise would be indescribable' (Thornbury, 1991:193). Furthermore, metaphors have power. As 'blueprints of thinking' (Martinez *et. al.*, 2001: 966) metaphors mark out not only the shape of our thoughts, but also the nature and scope of our action, in both creative and restrictive ways (*ibid*; Hudson, in Taylor, 1984). Analysis of the use of metaphor in talk about teaching and learning, from this perspective, seems to hold potential for understanding different articulations of the nature and meaning of learning in new ways.

In this analysis, participant talk was analysed in a general sense for occurrences of imagery and metaphor. In addition, the participants were asked directly, towards the end of the interview, if they could think of an image which summed up where they felt they were now in their lives. Both these images, and the use of metaphor overall, appeared to cluster into two main categories: expanding/enlarging, and tunnelling/climbing.

Expansion/enlarging

With the first group, metaphors of expansion, there were ideas of widening, broadening and moving outwards.

> I'm really looking forward to *widening*, widening my outlook on life (Graham)

183

> I think learning is *expansion* of the mind, to take in new things (Jack)

> Other people could always take things *further... really map things out*. Education to me means that you learn on a *broad*, a *wider* aspect. ... I think it enables you to think *laterally* (Shiela)

> I'm going to be wanting to know *the bigger picture* (Sandra)

There were also metaphors of roundness, completeness, and wholeness, as well as ideas of depth, clarification, opening and sharing.

> University is being taught at a different *level*. It's more *complete* – they've spent years doing it, they want to do it...it'll be a lot more enjoyable, because the *further down* you go, the more enjoyable it gets. Before you were taught at a *surface* level, just for an exam.... It gives you the grounding to learn the subject from *all directions*, to know the *round* picture, not just the surface (Sandra)

> I think (learning) makes you a much more *rounded* person... I would hope that learning takes away prejudices (Sheila)

> You know, when you wake up in the morning and you see daisies, they're really, really quite *clamped up*, and you're just waiting on that sunny day to come along and *open up*, because that's what I need to do... very much so, I do feel I need to *open up*... (Patricia)

One person in this group talked about making a new building from the rubble of a breakdown, another of feeling like a racing pigeon about to be let out, and a third of being like a dormant volcano about to erupt.

Tunnelling and climbing

Tunnelling and climbing represent a rather different orientation to starting university. For Will, who has been a security guard for the last 20 years, it is his life so far which is the tunnel:

> I could have done better at school... now I want to prove myself... get to a kind of *light* at the end of *the tunnel*. Now I'm in my 40s I feel I like I want to do something, catch up for previous years

For Jane, on the other hand, a 26 year old mother of four, university study itself is the tunnel:

> University is like a *mission*, you come out the end of the *tunnel* with your degree. It's a test to all of your senses... your social instincts... organising yourself

However, she also talks about 'loving' learning, which she describes as 'like a ladder, you go up every time you learn something'; the ladder will take her to where she wants to go in life. Sandra, a well-qualified nurse, uses metaphors of both expansion and climbing:

> I've *crossed the fence.* I was always on the other side of the fence looking over. Like you're an outsider.... and now I've crossed that fence. I'm still at the bottom of the field, ...but, I'm over the fence

Others use metaphors of height in the sense of 'rising above', or reaching up:

> Learning is also about *rising above* the knocks in life... not letting it *drag you down.* Learning at university is like, a *higher sphere...* there are brilliant minds at university (Jack)

When the participants' metaphors of learning are compared to those of the official discourse (Lillis, 2001) of Higher Education learning theory, (Prosser and Trigwell, 1999; Biggs, 1999; Entwistle, 2000; Prosser *et. al.*, 2003), a number of differences emerge (see table). The first is the difference between *deep* in the official discourse as individual, specialist knowledge, whilst in the participant discourses *deep* is related to ideas of expansion and growth in a multi-directional sense, connected to ideas of breadth and widening, as well as sharing and relationship with others. The second area of difference is in the idea of *progression upwards,* or *height.* In the mainstream discourse, the student is directed in an apparently straightforward, linear way, towards a clearly defined cognitive goal. Students who do not do this exhibit 'pathologies' or 'dissonance', leading to 'shallow' outcomes. In the participant discourse, movement is over, upwards and through, in the sense of battling against obstructions which can be social, relational and personal, and is directed towards brightness, light, new atmospheres, and new spaces for the imagination. The third contrast is the difference between learning as something of the *mind,* compared with learning as something involving a totality of *mind, body and being,* in a philosophical and ontological sense, for the participants. Finally, there is the contrast between the overall metaphors of *moulding* and *producing,* in relation to institutional agendas, compared to ideas of *expanding, clarifying, mapping, tunnelling and climbing* in relation to personal agendas. Learning in the first sense is constructed as a means for achieving institutional outcomes, whilst in

Metaphor comparison

Metaphors of the 'official discourse'	Metaphors used by participants
Deep and surface (approaches to learning) • Understanding the subject. • Subject in a lot of detail (specialist knowledge valued). • University learning task • Independent learning, autonomy	**Round and surface** • Enjoyable engagement with subject • Complete, round, whole – personal understanding of self and world • Relational – sharing knowledge, knowledge to help others

Moving upwards: hierarchy of conceptions of learning
• Articulated around one dimension (view of knowledge)
• Clear progression from one cognitive level to another
• Coherence between conception, approach, outcome
• Pathologies, dissonance, incoherence, confusion, aberrance, deviance, disintegration
	Width and opening, as well as depth
	• Branching out, thinking laterally, broader, wider
	• Mapping, answering questions about the world
	• Opening up
	
	Climbing over, battling through obstructions. Rising up to rarified atmospheres
	• Articulated around multiple dimensions, expressed in relation to life path
	  • A life that makes better sense (Jack, Sheila, Nigel)
	  • A life that is fairer (Will, Graham, Nigel)
	  • A life that has more (Sandra, Susan, Tim, Simon)
	  • A life that relates, that shares (Sandra, Graham)
	  • A life that gives me a job (Kathleen)
	• Struggle, challenge

Mind • Meaning as subject knowledge • Disembodied, de-contextualised	**Body, mind, and being** • Learning as an expression of desire • Learning as authoring the future • Learning as the creation of new kinds of being
Policy and institutional agendas: moulding and producing in an educational context • Which teaching approaches produce the better outcome? • How does assessment affect outcome?	**Personal agendas: enlarging, expanding, clarifying, opening, mapping in context of wider life** • HE learning as an answer to philosophical/ existential questions and desires

the second, it appears to be seen as a tool for the creation of new identities and selves.

Responding to the standard analysis

The comparison of metaphor types in these different discourses reveals aspects of these different conceptualisations of learning that might not be easy to see using other forms of analysis. Comparison in relation to types, or categories, creates space for new types of questions to be raised; in this case, for example, about the ways in which the institutional orientation towards learning, and the values associated with such learning, might differ significantly from the orientations and values of some mature learners. This makes possible further questions, perhaps in relation to the idea of fit between learners' orientations and those of the institution. Will those whose orientation is characterized by ideas of 'expansion', which appear to have some links to the top levels of the 'conceptions of learning' model in the official discourse[4], be more successful than those who express ideas of tunnelling and struggle, which institutional models do not acknowledge? And will the subject specialisation of disciplinary learning provide the broadening and opening of personal horizons that is hoped for, or will the narrowness of such knowledge-based specialisation lead perhaps to alienation, or disappointment?

However, discussion of the implications of this analysis beyond these questions, is potentially problematic. It could be argued that learner discourses are bound to be different from theoretical discourses because they have been generated in different ways, for different purposes. From this perspective, the 'official' picture of learning is a general abstraction, which should be used as an heuristic, rather than seen as a description of reality. The second picture, in this view, has been created from the accounts of a small group of individuals, and, as such, is problematic because it has limited applicability to other situations. What, those that argue in this way might ask, can the significance be of an analysis that relates to such a small sample of new learners in Higher Education?

This familiar question exhibits underpinning epistemological assumptions which reflect conceptions of scientific rigour, and habits of scientific analysis, which are so taken for granted that they are rarely commented upon. Cross-sectional analysis, resulting in the identification of categories (whether themes in qualitative data, or the results of factor analysis in more quantitative studies) is simply the way this kind of data analysis is usually done. This approach takes for granted that, in order to create a theme or category, a piece of the data has to be removed from the context in which it was originally expressed: to create a category such as 'metaphors of enlargement and expansion', for example, the metaphors have to be taken out of the narrative context within which they were originally located. This process of de-contextualisation, necessary in order to find themes in common across different accounts, is arguably not really consistent with contemporary awareness of the *context-specific* nature of phenomena, of the *locatedness* of things. In addition, theming and categorising are about creating patterns of *sameness*, which obscure and silence the ways in which things are *different*. Recent approaches to the study of learning, such as those based in theories such as social constructivism, situated learning, and some recent theoretical perspectives in adult education, Further Education and Higher Education express a concern with difference (as opposed to commonality), specificity (as opposed to generalisability), and the effects of context (as opposed to abstraction). The epistemology which underpins much research into learning does not seem to be congruent with these concerns.

One reason for this appears to be the power of the discourse of 'science' which underpins abstracting, generalising approaches. It is difficult to find different epistemologies which are able to compete with the power of this discourse, with which it might be possible to begin to create different kinds of understandings about learning. The deterministic and probabilistic assumptions which underpin many current constructions of educational research, however, are based on only one conception of science. There are other equally scientific epistemologies, such as those that underpin relativity, quantum, chaos and complexity theory. These types of theorising, although all different, are often underpinned by *non*-determinist assumptions, which have resulted in a range of different descriptions of fundamentally non-linear processes and patterns in phenomena.

These epistemologies have potential implications which are only just beginning to be explored in educational research. Complexity theory (Cilliers, 1998; Byrne, 1998), for example, points to the importance of *local interactions*, and to the *interconnectedness* of different elements in a local situation. This could be seen as focusing attention on the existence of many elements within individual contexts of learning which processes of abstraction and generalisation are forced to modify, in order to fit them into a category, or indeed, if they won't fit, to completely ignore. It also allows for recognition of a multiplicity of *connections* between elements, connections which have to be severed in theming and categorisation processes. From the perspective of theories of complexity and emergence, local elements constantly interact, and, through feedback, change and re-form each other in a continuing, non-linear, and unpredictable ways. This leads to the powerful and somewhat disturbing suggestion that meaningful order may be created by emergent processes which are fundamentally unpredictable, and untrackable.

The possible implications of some of these ideas in terms of data analysis is the focus of the research project from which this analysis is drawn. In terms of the data discussed above, it might be asked how the stories of the participants in this study would look if, instead of focusing upon creating themes out of groups of de-contextualised elements, different *local* elements of each story were looked at together, *without* necessarily any intention to try to articulate the precise nature of the relationships between these different elements?

Analysis in context: specificity, difference and the emergence of meaning

When the participants' use of metaphor is examined in relation to the different elements of each individual's story, there are two things which emerge in comparison to the analysis which underpins the first part of this chapter. The first is that the categories which can be created in a cross-sectional analysis (eg. metaphors of expansion or tunnelling) can no longer be sustained as discrete entities. In this second analysis, boundaries between categories refuse to be neatly drawn; categories mix and interweave, and constitute each other in ways that can only make sense in terms of the context within which the story is being told. Furthermore, the elements of the data which had been clustered together, suggesting the existence of a group of *like* phenomena (eg. 'expansion'), uncouple themselves into kaleidoscopic pictures of *difference* at the level of individual, contextualised constructions of meaning. Freed from the constraints of cross-sectional categorisation, however, patterns of meaning, so hard to sustain *across* different accounts, begin to emerge *within* accounts in quite clearly defined ways.

Jack

Jack (36) has mixed memories of school, which he left at 15, with no particular goal in mind. His father, a postman, died when he was 13. When he was about 17, his mother, who worked in a rubber works, fell ill, and from that time until the time of the interview he was her full-time carer. During this time he read a great deal. When his mother died, the year before the interview, Jack had a breakdown. Finding his way through this with the help of a counsellor, and influenced by his student nieces, Jack has emerged from this experience determined to become a historian. Considering that he has no school qualifications, and no post-school learning experience, he is extremely confident about this next step in his life

> I feel I'm ready to take on the world, actually... The whole thing I actually lacked over the course of my life was self-confidence... But now, I think it's just with the experience of last year, when my mother died, you know, ... em... I feel like, well, I've been able to take that on, overcome it, I feel I can take just about anything on.

> *So it's the experience of managing to live through that, and pick yourself up...*

> Exactly. The way I see it is like there's just a huge bomb that exploded, and there's just all the rubble that was left behind, you know, ... and ... then we cleared all the rubble away and just started building again, you know ... starting anew and afresh ... I'm renewed and reinvigorated

For Jack, learning is 'expansion of the mind to take in new ideas', and 'building up knowledge throughout life', both of which can happen either 'in the classroom' or in 'life in general'. He does differentiate between the two: classroom knowledge 'can help you with career prospects', whilst the other kind of learning is about 'rising above the knocks in life', such as the murder of a close relative, and the death of his mother. However, these two different aspects to learning are not necessarily separate:

> I suppose that's what I mean by academic learning, you're being taught by people, and you're sitting by people, who are being

taught with you, who are trying to learn the positive things in life. They're trying to do maybe some good, in life ... rather than experience the bad side...

Jack feels that there are 'people with brilliant minds' at university, and that being taught by them will make him 'even more intelligent':

...that's what I mean by expanded knowledge, your mind and that, opening up to new ideas, new situations, that kind of thing. I always feel its good to broaden the mind, take on new ideas...

This sense of renewal and expansion, however, incorporates a very practical goal. He wants to:

...get something better for myself out of life, you know. Maybe possibly a good career as a historian. That would be an excellent achievement.

Jack's apparently 'instrumental' focus on university as the path to a worthwhile career is pragmatic, philosophical, and ontological, all at the same time. University seems to be the start of a new way of *being*, which he hopes will make his experience of his existence more positive.

Sandra

Sandra (30s), who has negative memories of school, expresses these as frustration that her mother made her help with her catering business every day, rather than encouraging her to do school work. She suspects that her mother was jealous of her opportunities, after getting pregnant with Sandra when she was 16. Since school, Sandra, as a nurse, has done a whole range of professional courses, and is thus successful in educational terms. But this is not how she talks about her life. She is frustrated and desperate for change. Multiple things seem to have come together to make university seem important, and possible, now: a change of circumstances in returning from abroad to find unsatisfactory work, divorce, her child now at the age that it is possible to arrange childcare. In addition her sense of irritation with those she deems apathetic at work seems to have reached an intolerable level:

Five years ago I got a sense of learning being important, exciting. My husband loved his work, he used to get up at 4.00 am to study and enjoyed it. I've never felt that way. ...I want to know the big picture... people who are educated want to do their work, it comes across. I've seen that, in you, in other students, in my husband. Other people are just doing a job, complaining all the time...

Sandra talks about feeling up until now that she has never reached 'what she's supposed to be'. However, having got 'over the hurdle' of feeling 'small and insignificant' on her first day in the university, she nearly turned round and went home again, she now has clear, and strong, feelings about her current situation:

> I can feel it, this is the right place for me to be. It's a new feeling, bigger than getting married.....

> I've crossed the fence. I was always on the other side of the fence looking over. Like you're an outsider ... and now I've crossed that fence. I'm still at the bottom of the field, ...but, I'm over the fence.

> *What was the fence?*

> Just barriers, a lot of barriers, that you just go up against all the time, just in life, everything. And you just knew that there's more, and you're able to do more ... but you were always just held back. Whether its family, work, anything....

> *What do you see now that you're on the other side of the fence?*

> Eh... a lot of struggles, a lot of falling down...Yeah, I'm not in that house yet, and I've got a long way to go to get there.

> *So there's a house.*

> At the top of the field there's a house... And once I reach that house... I'll feel ... complete

Sandra uses images of 'completeness', as well as those of depth, height, hurdles and barriers. These different ideas are entwined together in complex ways. Apart from her own search for a kind of wholeness, for example, she talks about university learning as being both 'at a different level' and also 'more complete'. She talks of learning becoming more enjoyable 'the further *down* you go', and of her previous teachers teaching 'at a *surface* level', where no-one answered her questions. Despite her expressed lack of satisfaction with the formal learning she has done so far, her past engagement in professional courses involved more than simply a desire for professional advancement. She did extra courses because she wanted to know 'the *round* picture... from all directions' of her subject (she contrasts *round* with *surface*), so that she could 'help people as best as possible'. Like Jack, Sandra's view of learning at this stage is highly complex, involving existential, instrumental, intellectual and emotional desires which have coalesced at this point in her life into a sense of absolute clarity and determination. Her very personal, philosophical agenda, however, which seems to be characterised by wanting *more* of just about everything, is not only about herself, but incorporates relational and social desires.

Graham

Graham (30s) tells a different kind of story about alienation from his family, and from school experience. He moves schools, his dyslexia is misdiagnosed, he has an alcoholic teacher, and a stepfather, also a teacher, who is always comparing him negatively to his brother. In his teens, Graham seems to assert himself by resisting any Further Education; he fights the YTS mandatory college attendance and gets a special dispensation not to attend any classes. He eventually develops a liver problem from drinking. Trying to keep him out of the pubs, his mother, who works in a shop, buys him a historical novel. This chance intervention seems to change everything. It sparks an interest in history that links back to his grandfather, the one person he mentions being close to, who used to take him to Edinburgh castle. He begins to read more and more history, until his partner eventually persuades him, in his 30s, to do a university evening class. He finds the teacher inspiring, and begins to consider the possibility of studying history at university.

Currently working 12 hour shifts in a chicken farm, Graham is tired of not 'getting on' in life:

> (I'm looking forward to) Just a total change, of lifestyle, I think ... I'm just looking forward to ... being like everyone else, you know, sort of ... coming in, doing my work, enjoying what I'm doing, ... and then em ... having a little bit more time off, ... having a sort of brighter future...

Though again this could be categorised as an 'instrumental' desire to simply get a better job, Graham also talks about *widening* his current outlook on life, which he sees as *narrow*. For Graham, learning is about 'having knowledge that you wouldn't have in everyday life'; finding out what philosophy is, for example, and understanding politics. It is also about sharing what you learn with other people – colleagues who ask about Mary Queen of Scots, and tourists who want to know about Scotland. His dream is to work with visitors to Scotland, and perhaps to become an author. He talks of 'giving back' what you learn to others, and also about learning being 'nice and refreshing', compared with working on the chicken farm. Though he is terrified of losing his pay packet once he becomes a student, he has a clear image of where he is in his life at this point

> ...racing pigeons, when they're just getting let out... they can go anywhere, you know what I mean?

For Graham, learning at university appears to be the beginning of an attempt to reconstruct his place in the world, financially, socially, and existentially. Like both Jack and Sandra, learning incorporates simultaneously ideas of discovery, stimulation, and the possibility of a more satisfying work life. In contrast to many academic models, learning for Graham, as for Sandra, is also crucially connected to the ability to relate to others in specific ways, and indeed to the possibility of communicating with new groups and communities.

Looking at talk about learning in context also creates space for discussion of stories that cannot be forced into any kind of category. Patricia (43) for example, is coming into Higher Education with a paralysing fear of education that reaches back to her experience of an oppressive convent school in Ireland. She describes herself as waiting, like a blank sheet, trying to talk herself into positive thinking, wondering where university learning is going to take her. She wants to 'get the piece of paper' to verify her many years as an unqualified social worker, but she also hopes university learning will show her something in herself that others have seen in her, that she cannot see herself. Her image is of a field of clamped up daisies, waiting for the sun.

Rose (40s), after an adult life in journalism and horticulture, now wants to be a psychologist. Her definition of learning is 'joy', and her image is of a blackbird singing. Simon (30s), after a decade or so of running his own driving school, now wants to take the path that his parents persuaded him away from in his teens, towards becoming a biologist. Simon's definition of learning is 'getting and processing information relevant to the topic', in all situations, whether crossing the road or doing a degree, and his image is the cross on his printer test page. These orientations towards learning are characterised by difference, rather than similarity. Each person, seen within their own context, appears to be an 'exception' to the kinds of rules which might be created by other kinds of approach to analysis. Their exceptionality, however, cannot be said to be random or meaningless.

Conclusion

This chapter has used two types of analysis to explore metaphors in talk about learning in Higher Education. The focus on these two areas in the more conventional analysis raised a number of questions about the differences, and the similarities, between learner discourses and the official discourses of Higher Education learning theory. It was suggested that this analysis, whilst providing some useful insights, nonetheless created only one possible picture. Searching for a way in which it might be possible to illuminate more of the situated, located nature of learning, theories of complexity and emergence were introduced as a possible way of creating a different kind of framing. This approach appears to contain possibilities for the creation of a different kind of perspective on learning. Examining descriptions and metaphors in context suggested that each individual account of learning was characterised by *difference*, in contrast to the similarity groupings which emerged from the first analysis. The difference in metaphor and story, however, was not random or idiosyncratic at this individual level. Seen in relation to other elements of each participant's story, the use of description and metaphor was part of a patterning in each case which articulated something of the *meaning* of learning in Higher Education for each participant. Further exploration of this type of patterning could contain possibilities for the development of additional perspectives on Higher Educational learning, which might help to bring important aspects of learning out of the shadows inevitably cast by mainstream pedagogical theory (Rowland, 1993).

Notes

1   For a good overview of the original research in this area see Marton and Saljo, 1984/997.

2   The work of mainstream researchers in this area is also based on student perspectives, but these are largely elicited and theorised in relation to the specific conceptual framework described by the term 'phenomenography' (see Marton and Saljo, 1984/1997). The early work in this field did involve interviews, but student perspectives in many

contemporary versions of this tradition are often elicited by means of questionnaires rather than by talking to students themselves.

3   Access courses in Britain, run by both Further Education colleges, and by universities, provide a route into university for mature students who do not have standard entry qualifications.

4   The top layers of the 'conceptions of learning' model include learning as 'the abstraction of meaning', 'an interpretive process aimed at understanding reality', and 'developing as a person' (Marton and Saljo, 1984/997)

References

Biggs, J (1999) *Teaching for Quality Learning at University*. Buckingham: Open University Press

Bosma, H and Kunnen, E (eds) (2001) *Identity and Emotion*. Cambridge: Cambridge University Press

Byrne, D (1998) *Complexity Theory and the Social Sciences*. London: Routledge

Cilliers, P (1998) *Complexity and Post-modernism*. London: Routledge

Cullen, J Hadjivassiliou, K, Hamilton, E, Kelleher, J, Sommerlad, E and Stern, E (2002) *Review of Current Pedagogic Research and Practice in the Fields of Post-Compulsory Education and Lifelong Learning*. London: The Tavistock Institute

Entwistle, N (2000) Promoting deep learning through teaching and assessment: conceptual frameworks and educational contexts. Paper presented at the Teaching Learning and Research Project Annual Conference Leicester, November, 2000

Haggis, T (2003) Constructing images of ourselves? An investigation of 'approaches to learning' research in higher education, in *British Educational Research Journal* 29(1): 89-104

Haggis, T (forthcoming, 2004) Meaning, Identity, and 'Motivation': Expanding what matters in understanding learning in higher education?, in *Studies in Higher Education* 29(3)

HEFC (1999) *Institutional Learning and Teaching Strategies 99/55*, Bristol: Higher Education Funding Council

HEFC (2001) *Strategies for Learning and Teaching in Higher Education 01/37*, Bristol: Higher Education Funding Council

Light, G and Cox, R (2001) *Learning and Teaching in Higher Education*. London: Paul Chapman

Lillis, T (2001) *Student Writing*. London: Routledge

Martinez, M, Sauleda, N and Huber, G (2001) Metaphors as blueprints of thinking about teaching and learning, in: *Teaching and Teacher Education* 17, 965-977

Marton, F and Saljo, R (1984/1997) Approaches to learning, in: *The Experience of Learning*. Edinburgh: Scottish Academic Press

Prosser, M and Trigwell, K (1999) *Understanding learning and teaching*. Buckingham: Open University Press

Prosser, M, Ramsden, P, Trigwell, K and Martin, E, (2003) Dissonance in Experience of Teaching and its Relation to the Quality of Student Learning, in: *Studies in Higher Education* 28(1): 37–48

Rowland, S (1993) *The Enquiring Tutor: Exploring the Process of Learning.* London: Falmer Press

Savin-Baden, M (2000) *Problem-based Learning in Higher Education: Untold Stories.* Buckingham: Open University Press

Taylor, W (ed) *Metaphors of Education.* London: Heinemann

Thornbury, S (1991) Metaphors we work by: EFL and its metaphors, in: *English Language Teaching Journal* 45, 193-200

Contributors

Peter Ashworth is Professor of Educational Research in the School of Social Science and Law, Sheffield Hallam University, undertaking studies commissioned by the University into matters such as plagiarism, the admissions process, and the responsiveness of the University to ethnic minority cultures. Recent publications include work on master's education in nursing; the phenomenological notion of the lifeworld as a basis for qualitative research, and the implications for Higher Education of Hannah Arendt's educational views.

James Avis left school at the age of 16 and after working in retailing for a number of years studied for a degree in Management Science at the University of Manchester Institute of Science and Technology. He later taught Sociology in Further Education before moving to Oxford Brookes University where he was Educational Studies' course leader. He has since moved to the University of Wolverhampton where he is professor of Education Studies.

Tom Burns has taught media and sociology in FE and Learning Development at London Metropolitan University since the 1990s. Tom operates an educational consultancy and publishing company – Learning Curve Productions – which delivers INSET and which has produced *Everything you wanted to know about studying... but were too afraid to ask* and *The Work Smart Series of staff and student learning materials*. Most recently he has co-authored *Essential Study Skills: the complete guide to success @ university* for SAGE.

Jon Clark is Vice Principal of 'Osbourne' EBD School and a student on Sheffield's EdD programme. Throughout his career, Jon has worked in a wide range of Special Education contexts.

Sue Clegg is Professor of Educational Research and Head of Research in the Learning and Teaching Institute, Sheffield Hallam University.

She works on a wide range of projects with staff in schools exploring practice, and on policy issues. Recent publications include work on racialising discourses in Higher Education, the implementation of learning and teaching policies, problematising e-learning, and critical approaches to reflective practice. She is currently working on the issue of personal development planning.

Kathryn Ecclestone is Senior Lecturer in Post-Compulsory Education at the University of Exeter. Kathryn started an education career working with unemployed young people in the Youth Opportunities Programmes in the late 1970s. Until the early 1990s, she taught and managed Vocational Education and Access to Higher Education programmes in Further Education. Since 1993, she has worked in post-16 teacher education and professional development. Her research and teaching interests are in assessment policy, ideology and practice and learner autonomy.

Julie Evans was recently appointed as a lecturer in Sociology at the College of St Mark and St John in Plymouth. Prior to this Julie has worked on a range of research projects and last year she was a Research Fellow on an ESRC funded project working within Early Years Education in mid-Devon. Julie successfully completed her PhD in 2002, which focused on social inequalities, gender and young children's relationships with contemporary consumer culture.

Tamsin Haggis is a lecturer in Lifelong Learning in the Institute of Education at the University of Stirling. Her main teaching responsibilities involve working with teachers in the Further Education sector on the Scottish TQ(FE). Her research interests include a variety of issues connected with learning in Higher Education. These include the connection between research methodology and the theorisation of learning, academic literacies, and the implications of mass Higher Education for traditional cultures of university learning.

Roger Harrison is a lecturer in the Centre for Educational Policy Leadership and Lifelong Learning at the Open University. He has written open learning courses at pre-undergraduate, undergraduate and postgraduate level for adult learners and professionals engaged in the education of adults. His research includes theoretical and empirical studies on the formation of learner and professional identities in education, on informal learning, and guidance and counselling in learning. He is a regular contributor to national and international conferences and has published widely through journals and other academic texts

Debbie Holley is a senior lecturer in Purchasing and Supply Chain Management in the Department of Business and Service Sector management at London Metropolitan University. She researches student attitudes to learning and is interested in the use of technology to motivate students. Debbie holds the departmental role of Learning Support Strategist, developing and implementing strategies to enable students to maximise their potential. For further information, please visit her website, http://homepages.unl.ac.uk/holleyd

Patti Lather is a Professor in the Cultural Studies in Education Program at the School of Educational Policy and Leadership at Ohio State University where she teaches qualitative research in education and gender and education. She is the author of two books, forty-seven articles, reviews and book chapters and has delivered more than sixty invited keynote addresses and lectures around the world. Her book *Getting Smart: Feminist research and pedagogy with/in the postmodern* received a 1991 Critics Choice Award. *Troubling the Angels: Women living with HIV/AIDS*, co-authored with Chris Smithies, received a 1998 CHOICE Award as one of the best academic books of the year. She has chapters in the *Handbook of Research on Teaching* (V. Richardson, ed., 2001), *Working the Ruins: Feminist Theory and Methods in Education* (E. St. Pierre and W. Pillow, eds, 2000) and *The Handbook of Ethnography* (P. Atkinson et al, eds, 2001). She is presently working on a manuscript, *Getting Lost: Working the Ruins of Feminist Methodology.*

Wendy Martin is a senior lecturer in the Faculty of Education at the University of Plymouth. Her interests lie in research methodology and in the experiences of mature students entering HE.

Professor Mike Newby is Dean of the Faculty of Education at the University of Plymouth. From 1998 to 2001 he was Chair of the Universities Council for the Education of Teachers (UCET). Having been an English teacher in school and in the FE sector, he has worked in teacher education since the early 1970s and has been a senior manager in HE, first in Wales and now in the west country, since 1985.

Valerie Reardon. After graduating as a mature student, Valerie Reardon began teaching at Falmouth College of Arts and has published widely on contemporary art and artists. Her doctoral thesis on the collages of Hannelore Baron further developed her interest in psychoanalytic, postcolonial and postmodern understandings of identity. She recently spent two years at Cornwall College as a lecturer in Post-Compulsory Education where she researched into media representations of teachers and the formation of teacher identities. She is currently Head of Media Studies/Art and Design at The College of St Mark and St John.

Pat Sikes is a senior lecturer and Director of the EdD programme at the School of Education at the University of Sheffield. She is Series Editor of the Open University series *Doing Qualitative Research in Educational Settings* and her most recent publications include Sikes, Nixon and Carr (Eds) (2003) *The Moral Foundations of Educational Research* Maidenhead, Open University/McGraw Hill.

Sandra Sinfield has worked in Further and Higher Education since 1980 – with a special focus on the 'non-traditional' student on A'level, Access, undergraduate and postgraduate programmes. Now senior lecturer: Co-ordinator for Learning Development (North Campus) at London Metropolitan University, Sandra has worked with Tom Burns both at Learning Curve and in Learning Development research and delivery at London Met and with Debbie Holley on student support issues. She is co-author with Tom Burns of *Essential Study Skills: the complete guide to success @ university.*

Ian Stronach is Research Professor of Education at the Institute of Education, MMU. He is also a current Editor of the *British Educational Research Journal*. His research interests include evaluation, cultural theory, and action research. Current topics include the nature of research-based knowledge, the future of action research and evaluation, and the nature of professionalism.

Index

203

HOW TO
STRENGTHEN
YOUR
FAITH